The Twentieth-Century Pentecostal Explosion

The Exciting Growth of Pentecostal Churches and Charismatic Renewal Movements

VINSON SYNAN

Creation House
Altamonte Springs, Florida

Creation House
Strang Communications Company
190 N. Westmonte Drive
Altamonte Springs, FL 32714
(305) 869-5005

This book is dedicated to David Sklorenko, director, and the members of the planning committee of the New Orleans Congresses on the Holy Spirit and World Evangelization: Pepe Alonzo, Bill Beatty, Larry Christenson, Ithiel Clemmons, Charles Green, Jane Hansen, Charles Irish, Jim Jackson, Bob Mendolsohn, Kevin Ranaghan, Vernon Stoop Jr., Karl Strader and Bob Weiner.

Contents

Introduction

In writing this book, I was aware that some readers might ask the question, Why another book on Pentecostal/charismatic history by Vinson Synan? After all, I have already published seven historical works on this subject and this one is the eighth. My previous ones include: *Emmanuel College: The First Fifty Years* (1968); *The Holiness Pentecostal Movement in the United States* (1971); *The Old-Time Power: A History of the Pentecostal Holiness Church* (1973); *Aspects of Pentecostal/Charismatic Origins* (1974); *Charismatic Bridges* (1974); *Azusa Street* (1976); and *In the Latter Days* (1984). Yet after writing these histories, I find that there is still a great deal that remains to be told about this movement.

Perhaps a few words of explanation would be in order. This book came into being as a result of the New Orleans Congresses on the Holy Spirit and World Evangelization held in the Superdome in 1986 and 1987. Since I served as chairman of these great gatherings, my travels took me to many of the churches and conventions of the supporting groups. I learned much about these charismatic renewal groups in the course of my travels. I was also able to interview many of the pioneer leaders firsthand about their own stories. They in turn were able to read my manuscripts and offer many suggestions as to facts and interpretation.

In addition to these opportunities, Bert Ghezzi of Strang Communications urged me to write a series of articles for *Charisma* magazine giving the histories of the major groups sponsoring the congresses. As Ghezzi suggested, my relationships with many of the leaders and pioneers of these movements in the course of my work would be the opportunity of a lifetime to gather primary source materials for the series and a book that would follow.

As I began work on the series, it became clear that many of the mainline charismatic renewal groups had never had a narrative history written giving basic data on their origins and development. Therefore, in order to write these articles, I was forced to do research into primary sources including periodicals published by the various groups. I also had the privilege of interviewing personally many of the persons involved in the pioneering phases of the organizations. This amounted to plowing new ground, historically speaking.

I was especially intrigued with the rare opportunities I had to talk with such persons as Richard Winkler, Harald Bredesen, Dennis Bennett, Gerald Derstine, James Brown, Larry Christenson, Kevin Ranaghan, David du Plessis and many others. These men were spiritual revolutionaries in their time and will undoubtedly go down in history as some of the important Christian leaders of this century.

For some of the chapters, the task was quite easy.

Several denominations already have well-written histories that pass the tests of historical and scholarly accuracy. These include many of the classical Pentecostal groups such as the Assemblies of God and the Catholic charismatic renewal movement. Much of the information about these groups was previously printed in books that I and others have already published. These were twice-told tales, so to speak. In some cases, however, I was able to add some information from original sources in these chapters also.

The most important contribution of this volume, therefore, will be the chapters on the movements that have never been told before in one narrative. To my knowledge, until now the histories of many renewal movements have not been written and published, although parts of the stories were published in various periodicals and autobiographies.

Because of time and space restraints, it was not possible to tell the stories of all the other Pentecostal and charismatic renewal groups that by all rights also deserve to be treated in this volume. Among the classical Pentecostal groups in this category would be the Pentecostal Church of God, the United Pentecostal Church, the Open Bible Standard Church, the Pentecostal Freewill Baptist Church and the United Holy Church. In addition to these, there are scores of smaller Pentecostal denominations whose stories need to be told.

Furthermore, I am not dealing here with the large number of new indigenous Third World Pentecostal churches and denominations in Africa, Asia or Latin America which numbered some 34 million persons in 1985. The stories of these movements and their leaders also await a historian who will record their histories for posterity. Their founders and leaders have stories every bit as exciting and important as those of Dennis Bennett and others in America.

There are also emerging coalitions of non-denominational groups that are fast becoming major forces in the overall renewal picture. Among these would be the National Leadership Conference led by Jim Jackson of Montreat, North Carolina; the Network of Christian Ministries led by Charles Green of New Orleans; and the Charismatic Bible Ministries led by Oral Roberts of Tulsa, Oklahoma. Associated with these groups are some of the vital and fast-growing "faith" and "Word" churches influenced by Kenneth Hagin and Kenneth Copeland. These groups, moreover, are bringing together literally thousands of independent charismatic congregations who are not related to any denomination, mainline or Pentecostal.

Noteworthy also are the stories of such special interest groups as the charismatic Messianic Jewish believers; the Maranatha Christian Churches, led by Bob Weiner, which concentrate on campus ministries; and Youth With a Mission (YWAM), a ministry of short-term missionaries led by Loren Cunningham of Hawaii. Also waiting to be told is the story of Associated International Mission Services (AIMS), the new missions organization formed to serve the vast number of independent charismatic and Pentecostal congregations not already served by established mission agencies.

The chapters have been arranged in alphabetical order on purpose, since it is the conviction of the writer that they all are expressions of the same historic movement. Just as there is only one Holy Spirit, there is only one outpouring of the Holy Spirit in the churches. The book also does not follow a chronological order of historic development.

The following classification will situate them in their proper historical and theological milieus:

The Classical Pentecostals

These include the older Pentecostal denominations that owe their origins to the nineteenth-century Holiness and higher life movements which culminated in the "initial evidence" theory of Charles Parham in 1901 and William J. Seymour at Azusa Street in 1906. This teaching held that the first evidence of the baptism in the Holy Spirit was to speak in tongues. Although several theological and organizational differences have developed between these groups during the century, they are here considered as integral components of one historical movement.

These are reformation groups in that they were "reformed" into new denominations after 1901 when their people were rejected from the mainline churches.

These groups include:

The Assemblies of God

The Churches of God

The Church of God in Christ

The International Church of the Foursquare
  Gospel

The Pentecostal Holiness Church

Although these are but a fraction of the thousands of classical Pentecostal groups in the world, they are the oldest of the North American bodies. Most of them have developed elaborate denominational structures and have distinguished themselves by sending missionaries to found flourishing missions branches in most of the nations of the world.

Taken together, the classical Pentecostals now constitute the largest family of Protestant Christians in the world. In 1985, for instance, together with Third World indigenous Pentecostal denominations, they numbered about 60 million persons worldwide. By far, they also are the fastest growing churches in the world.

The Charismatic Renewal Movements

The second group constitutes those renewal groups which have been known by the term charismatic since 1970. These groups developed after 1960 and were first called neo-Pentecostals. They accept all the charismata as valid for today, while disagreeing with the classical Pentecostals that speaking in tongues (glossolalia) is the necessary first sign of receiving the baptism in the Holy Spirit. Intensely loyal to their own church traditions, they are attempting to integrate the renewal into their own church's theology and ecclesiology. They generally see the charismatic renewal as a great sign of hope for the future life and growth of their churches.

These groups are as follows:
The Baptist Renewal
The Catholic Charismatic Renewal
The Churches of Christ Renewal
The Episcopal Renewal
The Lutheran Renewal
The Mennonite Renewal
The Methodist Renewal
The Orthodox Renewal
The Presbyterian Renewal
The United Church of Christ Renewal
The Wesleyan-Holiness Renewal

In a real sense, these are part of the same Pentecostal movement that has been sweeping the churches since the beginning of the century. They differ from their classical Pentecostal co-religionists more in style than in substance. Taken together, these movements constitute the most important force to challenge Christianity since the Reformation. The statistics of growth are staggering indeed.

According to David Barrett, editor of the *World Christian Encyclopedia*, the Pentecostals had surpassed all the Protestant Reformation families of churches by 1980. In addition to these Pentecostal Christians, the charismatic movement had entered all the traditional churches of Christendom. In his projections for the future, Barrett estimated the following figures of world Christianity for the year 1985:

World Christian Encyclopedia

World population	About 5 billion persons

I. Of major world religions in 1985

Christians	1,548 million
Muslims	817 million
Hindus	647 million
Buddhists	295 million
Jewish	18 million

II. Of Christians

Roman Catholics	884 million
Protestant	360 million
Eastern Orthodox	170 million
Third World indigenous	95 million
Marginal Christians	16 million

III. Of Protestants

Denominational Pentecostals	58,999,900
A. Classical Pentecostals	24,800,000
B. Indigenous Pentecostals	34,200,000
Anglicans	51,100,100

Baptists	50,321,900
Lutherans	44,900,000
Presbyterians	43,445,500
Methodists	31,717,500
Holiness (Non-Pentecostal)	6,091,700
Mormons	4,475,500

IV. Of Pentecostals

Denominational Pentecostals	58,999,900
Active Charismatics	16,800,000
Inactive Protestant Charismatics	40,000,000
Inactive Catholic Charismatics	43,000,000
Chinese Pentecostals (Sui Generis)	19,000,000
Total Pentecostal Charismatic Christians in 1985	177,800,000

These projections indicate that in 1985 over ten percent of all the Christians in the world were of the Pentecostal or charismatic type. Barrett projects a rate of growth to the end of the century which will place the number of Pentecostals and charismatics at 300 million persons, or fifteen percent of world Christians. This projection is all the more remarkable when one considers that before January 1, 1901, this category of Christians did not even exist.

Another astounding fact revealed by the above figures is the huge number of "inactive" Catholic and Protestant charismatics who have at one time or another been involved with the movement. Those Barrett defined as "active" were the ones who attended prayer meetings and participated regularly on a weekly basis in some charismatic activity.

Evidently there are many "graduates" of the charismatic movement who are either serving in their churches in some capacity other than specifically charismatic activities, or who have dropped out of the movement for various reasons. This fact should be of great concern to the leaders of the various charismatic renewal movements.

Studies have shown that large numbers of charismatics move on to places of ministry and service within their churches which removed them from their former activities. In practically all denominations, charismatics are serving as pastors, priests, teachers, lay leaders and the like. In a way this demonstrates the fact that the renewal has been moving into the lifeblood of the churches just as Cardinal Suenens suggested several years ago.

On the following pages, you will be introduced to the people who pioneered this movement in this century. They are truly spiritual revolutionaries. The church of Jesus Christ owes them a debt that it will never be able to repay. Because of them, the church will never be the same again!

CHAPTER ONE

The Assemblies of God

With more than 16 million members worldwide, the Assemblies of God is by far the largest and best-known Pentecostal fellowship on this planet. It is also the most influential and visible Pentecostal body, commanding respect in the broader world of evangelical and charismatic Christianity.

The history of the Assemblies of God is in large part the story of the entire Pentecostal movement, not only in the United States, but also around the world. With roots in the apostolic faith movement, founded by Charles Parham, and the Azusa Street revival, it was the first denomination to be entirely a product of the Pentecostal movement. The other earlier Pentecostal bodies had roots in the Holiness movement.

In April 1914, more than 300 persons gathered in the Grand Opera House in Hot Springs, Arkansas, to create a new national organization for the hundreds of independent Pentecostal assemblies that dotted the cities and towns across the country. This meeting was to be an important turning point for the Pentecostal movement in the United States and ultimately for the world.[1]

Formation of the Assemblies of God

The formation of this new fellowship owed much to men who were not present in Hot Springs and who were never to be a part of the church. Included in this number were Charles Parham, the formulator of the teaching that speaking in tongues was the "initial evidence" of the baptism in the Holy Spirit, a doctrine which became the distinctive of the Assemblies of God belief concerning the baptism in the Holy Spirit. Another absentee was William J. Seymour who led the Azusa Street revival in Los Angeles which influenced most of those present to accept the experience. A third person, William Durham, who had passed away in 1912, forged the most distinctive doctrine of the new denomination, the "finished work" theory of entire sanctification which distinguished the Assemblies of God from the older Holiness-Pentecostal bodies which stressed the "second work" aspect of sanctification. The fourth absentee was A.B. Simpson, founder of the Christian and Missionary Alliance, whose church furnished many of the leaders of the new church as well as its basic theology and world missions thrust.[2]

Another who was present but who did not join was Charles H. Mason, head of the Church of God in Christ from Memphis, Tennessee. Though Mason was black and most of the members of his church were blacks, a significant number were whites. Many of those forming the Assemblies of God were white pastors who had been affiliated with Mason and his church. Many had carried credentials of the Church of God in Christ provided by Mason under a "gentleman's agreement" that none would be issued to anyone who was "unworthy."

Though the ties between Mason and the white Pentecostals were not strong by 1914, Mason was nevertheless invited to preach at the convention. He did not join the new church, however. In a sense, the organization of the Assemblies of God was in part a racial separation from Mason's church.[3]

Founding Fathers

Those who were present at the Hot Springs Council represented the major elements that formed the church. The chairman and first general superintendent was Eudorus N. Bell, pastor of a local Pentecostal assembly in Malvern, Arkansas, who had been educated in the Southern Baptist Seminary in Louisville, Kentucky, and who had studied at the University of Chicago. Many Baptists such as he had entered into the Pentecostal experience despite the lack of teaching in the Holiness tradition. Bell represented the large "baptistic" element of the new church.[4]

J. Roswell Flower was elected to serve as general secretary of the church at the youthful age of 26. He was to serve in many positions in the Assemblies of God until his retirement in 1959, when he was again in the position of general secretary. Flower, along with Noel Perkin and Frank Boyd, had been loosely associated with the Christian and Missionary Alliance before entering the Pentecostal ranks.[5]

M.M. Pinson, an ardent follower of William Durham, preached the keynote sermon at the council on "the finished work of Calvary," the dominant theological theme of the gathering. Pinson had been ordained in J.O. McClurkan's Pentecostal Mission in Nashville, Tennessee, a group that later merged with the Church of the Nazarene. He represented the large number of

Wesleyans who joined the Assemblies despite the newer view on sanctification. Indeed, thousands of Holiness-Pentecostals representing various views of holiness joined with the Assemblies in the next decade. Thus, during these years, one of the most controversial questions in the church's official periodical, *The Pentecostal Evangel*, concerned the second blessing.[6]

Pinson, Flower and Bell also edited the three periodicals which influenced the call to Hot Springs. Flower's *Christian Evangel* was published in Plainfield, Indiana. Bell's *Apostolic Faith* and Pinson's *Word and Witness*, which had been merged under the latter name in 1912, were published in Malvern, Arkansas.[7]

In their roles of communicating church news and upcoming conventions, these periodicals were vital to the development of the basic organizations that came together in Hot Springs to form the new church. In Alabama, Pinson's group used the name Church of God from 1909 until 1911 when it changed its name to Church of God in Christ. Bell's group in Texas had used the name Apostolic Faith until 1911 when it also adopted the name Church of God in Christ and accepted credentials from Mason's church. These two groups joined with Flower in Indiana by issuing the call for the Hot Springs council in 1914. Others joining them in the call were A.P. Collins, H.A. Goss and D.C.O. Opperman.[8]

Reasons for Organizing

Five reasons were given for the call to hold the Hot Springs council. The first was to formulate a defensible doctrinal position for the growing number of independent Pentecostal churches which were often tossed about "with every wind of doctrine." A second reason was the desire to consolidate and conserve the Pentecostal work, which was in danger of dissipating without better mutual support from pastors who were often isolated from each other and lacking in fellowship.

A third reason was the need for a central foreign missions agency which could account for funds being sent abroad to the host of eager Pentecostal missionaries who were fanning out all over the world with little experience, support or direction. A fourth reason was the need to establish approved Bible schools to train future pastors and leaders for the churches.

A fifth reason for the council grew out of the first four. A new organization was needed to conserve the fruit of the Pentecostal revival that was moving powerfully throughout the nation and the world. What was produced in Hot Springs was a "new wineskin" for the new wine of the Holy Spirit that was being poured out.[9]

The Teachings of the Church

The name for the new church was fundamental to its success. Since the name common to most of the groups coming together was the Church of God in Christ, the new name conveyed a variation of that name. The word "assembly" comes from the same Greek word that is commonly translated "church." The plural form "assemblies" pointed to the congregational nature of the group which consisted of hundreds of independent assemblies banded together for fellowship and common ministry. The name was suggested by T.K. Leonard, whose local congregation in Findlay, Ohio, had been called Assembly of God for several years before 1914.[10]

There was a common concern that the new church

should not be a creedal one and not too tightly organized. Therefore it was decided that a binding creedal statement of faith would not be adopted. However, the Preamble and Resolution on Constitution contained the basic teachings on which the churches agreed, thus placing them in the non-Wesleyan, evangelical, dispensational Pentecostal camp. The crucial doctrine which held all together was that speaking in tongues was the "initial evidence" of the baptism in the Holy Spirit.[11]

The doctrinal latitude allowed in 1914 was an effort to continue the freedom of the Spirit to move in fresh ways in the churches. Any doctrinal restraints that would inhibit this freedom were to be avoided. This cherished freedom was to be severely tested, however, by the rise of the "oneness" movement in the church during the next two years.

This movement, which supporters called the "Jesus Name" movement and detractors dubbed the "Jesus Only" movement, had origins in California in 1913, just one year before the meeting of the Hot Springs council. Led by Frank Ewart and Glen Cook, the new teaching denied the doctrine of the Trinity and insisted on a unitarianism of the Son. Trinitarians were accused of worshipping "three gods." The oneness view was that the only valid form of water baptism was "in Jesus' name" and that speaking in tongues was necessary to salvation. This teaching spread rapidly from assembly to assembly after 1914 and threatened to engulf the entire church.[12]

The danger was heightened in 1915 when the general superintendent, Bell, was rebaptized in Jesus' name. The Third General Council, which convened in St. Louis, Missouri, in October 1915, was so divided that no vote was taken on the explosive new issue. In the following months the trinitarians, led by Flower, Pinson and John W. Welch, rallied their forces to counter the unitarians. A crucial victory was the reconversion of Bell to the trinitarian view. By the time the Fourth General Council convened in 1916, the trinitarians were in control. When the final vote was taken, the new denomination lost 156 of its ordained ministers to the Jesus' name partisans.

With this decision behind them, the remaining delegates then adopted a trinitarian statement of faith which became the doctrinal standard of practically all the Pentecostal churches formed after that time.[13]

The Church Grows

The growth of the Assemblies of God since 1914 has been phenomenal, both in the United States and around the world. Begun basically as a missionary society, the church developed one of the most aggressive foreign missions programs in the world. Missionaries were sent to the far corners of the globe to spread the Pentecostal message. Sacrificial giving for world missions became the major concern of the churches.

The desire to expand in the mission fields was matched by an equal desire to spread throughout the United States. Assemblies of God churches were soon planted in every state of the union. In large cities where the mainline churches were dying, thriving assemblies were organized. In thousands of cities where other denominations failed, the Assemblies of God was able to penetrate.

The greatest growth of the Assemblies of God came after World War II in the healing revivals that brought the Pentecostal message to the masses of the nation. After a period of slower growth in the 1960s, the church again prospered in the period of the charismatic renewal in the traditional denominations. The 1970s and first half of the 1980s saw the church grow to become one of the major denominations in the United States. By 1985 some of the largest congregations in the nation were affiliated with the Assemblies of God. Among them were Karl Strader's Carpenter's Home Church in Lakeland, Florida, with a sanctuary seating about 10,000 persons. Other large assemblies include the 6,000-seat Crossroads Cathedral, Oklahoma City, Oklahoma, pastored by Dan Sheaffer; Calvary Temple in Irving, Texas, pastored by Don George; and First Assembly of God in Phoenix, Arizona, pastored by Tommy Barnett.[14]

Leading the world in size and church growth is the Assemblies of God church in Seoul, South Korea, led by Paul Yonggi Cho. It is known locally as the Yoido Full Gospel Church. With a membership of more than 550,000 in 1986, this congregation is expected to pass the one million mark by 1990.[15]

The growth statistics of the Assemblies of God are impressive indeed. From the 300 members who gathered in Hot Springs in 1914, the church has grown to a worldwide adherency of over 16 million persons (three times the size of the Mormon Church), of which 2.3 million are in the United States. These Christians worship in a global community of 121,424 churches and outreach centers, including 10,886 in the United States. A total of 1,464 American missionaries work in 118 countries. Around the world 301 Bible schools train ministers to spread the work of the church.[16]

When the missions program was started it was decided that the goal of the church was to develop self-governing, self-supporting fields—free of dependence on the church in the United States. Therefore many national churches carry the name Assemblies of God without direct ties to the American headquarters in Springfield, Missouri. Though all fly the same banner and agree on the same doctrines, throughout the world they are more truly a fellowship of national, independent churches than a single international church body. This is true of the largest national church, the Brazilian Assemblies of God. The Brazilian church was formed in 1910, four years before the one in the United States.

Of all the leaders in the history of the Assemblies of God, none has exerted a more far-reaching influence than Thomas Zimmerman, who ended his service as general superintendent in December 1985. During his 26 years in office, the church more than doubled in size in the United States. Zimmerman also helped bring the Pentecostals into the evangelical mainstream when he was elected as the first Pentecostal president of the National Association of Evangelicals. After the 1985 general council, he was asked to serve as president of the Lausanne committee.[17]

In the 1980s members of the Assemblies of God attained high positions in the political world. James Watt, who served as secretary of the interior under President Reagan, was the first Pentecostal ever to hold a position of cabinet rank. In 1985 John D. Ashcroft was inaugurated as governor of Missouri, the first Pentecostal to be elected governor of a state.

Traveling almost anywhere in the world, one is likely to see congregations of the Assemblies of God in the smallest village or the most densely populated metropolis.

For more information on the Assemblies of God, write to:
Office of Information
The Assemblies of God
1445 Boonville Avenue
Springfield, MO 65802
(417) 862-2781

CHAPTER TWO

The Baptist Renewal

John Osteen was a typical Southern Baptist pastor in 1958 with a grave problem in his family. His daughter, who had been born with cerebral palsy, was given no hope of recovery by her doctors. In desperation, this man, pastor of the Hibbard Memorial Baptist Church in Houston, Texas, began to study the promises of divine healing in the Bible. With an awakened interest in the miracles recorded in the New Testament, he prayed for his daughter, and to his happy astonishment, she was healed miraculously.

Shortly after this, Osteen sought the fellowship of Pentecostals in the Houston area. J.R. Godwin, pastor of Houston's First Assembly of God, befriended him and explained to him the baptism in the Holy Spirit. In a short time, Osteen received a powerful Pentecostal experience "with a flow of tongues."

A few months later, the Hibbard Baptist Church conducted a trial, charging Osteen with "heresy." During the time of the trial, two deacons who had opposed him also spoke in tongues and switched sides. At the end of the trial, 82 percent of the congregation voted in Osteen's favor. Although he was allowed to stay at the church, he was often heckled by his opponents. Finally, in 1961, he and 100 of his supporters moved their services to a local feed and seed store where they organized the Lakewood Baptist Church.

After two years in the new location, Osteen heard the Lord tell him to "lift up your voice like an archangel and prophesy to my people in the valley of dry bones." This led to several years of evangelistic crusades in many parts of the world with amazing results. In 1969, he was led to return to the Lakewood church and resume his pastorate there. He again started with about 100 people. Today, the Lakewood congregation numbers over 5,000 families and ministers regularly to 15,000 people per week.[1]

In many ways, Osteen's story is the story of the charismatic renewal movement among Baptists. He is one of untold hundreds of Baptist pastors who have been renewed in the Holy Spirit in recent years and have suffered varying degrees of rejection from their churches.

The Baptists

Baptists make up one of the Protestant families of churches which have roots in the "Radical Reformation" of the sixteenth century. On the European continent, they were first called Anabaptists because they insisted on rebaptizing converts by total immersion. Because of their radical teachings, which at one time included polygamy among the German "Muenster" Baptists, early Anabaptists were persecuted by both Catholics and Reformers alike.[2]

In England, Baptist churches spread across the country during the seventeenth century, especially during the time of Cromwell's Puritan revolution. During this time, two major streams of Baptist thought emerged. The Particular Baptists followed a strict Calvinist view of predestination, while the General Baptists adhered to a more Arminian "free will" view of salvation. In time, the more Calvinist branch planted the first Baptist congregations in the American colonies.[3]

The first well-known Baptist in America was Roger Williams who was banished from Massachusetts to Rhode Island in 1634 for opposing the teachings of the dominant Congregationalist church. His plea was for religious liberty and freedom of conscience. In 1636 Williams founded the Rhode Island colony as a refuge for Baptists, Quakers and other dissenters who suffered persecution for their religious beliefs. In 1639 he founded the first Baptist congregation in America in Providence, Rhode Island.[4]

In the following years, indigenous Baptist congregations were planted in all of the colonies. For the most part, Baptists ministered to the common people. In some colonies, they were persecuted by the established churches, especially in Massachusetts and in the Southern colonies. For example, in eighteenth-century Virginia, Baptists were forbidden to preach without licenses from the established Anglican churches. On one occasion after they had been thrown in jail, the Baptist pastors of Chesterfield County preached to their congregations through their prison bars.

Baptist Beliefs

In general, Baptists have held to several basic beliefs, although they have always claimed to be a non-creedal church with no binding statements of faith. The most authoritative source of doctrine for American Baptists in the London Confession of 1689 which was adopted substantially by American Baptists in the Philadelphia Confession of 1742. Generally, most Baptists in the world would support the following six basic principles:

1. The supremacy of the Bible
2. Believer's baptism by immersion only
3. Churches composed only of believers
4. The priesthood of all believers
5. Congregational church government
6. Separation of church and state

The foregoing statements place the Baptists in the mainstream of evangelical Protestantism. Although there are important doctrinal differences between Baptists and other Protestant groups such as Methodists and Presbyterians, there are few major differences in their liturgies.[5]

Largely absent from modern Baptist doctrinal formulations are any mention of signs and wonders or the gifts of the Spirit. Some early Baptist statements seem to indicate an openness to manifestations of the Spirit, however. From England early American Baptists received a tradition of laying on of hands after water baptism "for a further reception of the Holy Spirit of promise, or for the addition of the grace of the Spirit..." for "the whole Gospel was confirmed in primitive times by signs and wonders and divers miracles and gifts of the Holy Ghost in general." Baptist historian Edward Hiscox points to early records of the Philadelphia association where there are indications that various gifts of the Spirit were in operation in the churches of that area about 1743.[6]

Through the years, however, the doctrine of the laying on of hands fell into disuse in the churches. Though there seems to be evidence of charismatic activity among some early Baptists, in time the vast majority of the pastors and teachers in the churches adopted a "cessation of the charismata" view of the gifts which was common in most churches. By the twentieth-century, the most common argument heard in Baptist churches was that the signs and wonders of the Bible were meant only for the apostolic age.

Despite this trend, several prominent nineteenth-century Baptists voiced expectations of a restoration of apostolic signs and wonders to the church. Such well-known Baptist leaders as C.H. Spurgeon in London and A.J. Gordon in Boston often preached about a new out-pouring of the Holy Spirit in their day that would radically change the church and the world. Indeed, Gordon, a leading turn-of-the-century Baptist pastor and teacher, is often cited as a forerunner of modern Pentecostalism because of his forceful teachings on a "baptism in the Holy Spirit" subsequent to conversion and the reality of divine healing in answer to prayer.[7]

These men were the exceptions to the rule, however. Coming from the Calvinist tradition, Baptists have generally been less affected by perfectionist and charismatic movements, most of which have generally had their roots in the Arminian-Wesleyan tradition. Yet, in the twentieth century, the Pentecostal churches have probably won more converts from among Baptists than from any other Protestant group in the United States.

Early Baptist Pentecostals

Though Osteen was an early neo-Pentecostal, he was by no means the first Baptist in America to be numbered among the Pentecostals. That distinction is held by a group of Freewill Baptists in North and South Carolina who received the "baptism" and spoke in tongues after the Azusa Street outpouring in 1906. Hearing the Pentecostal message in Dunn, North Carolina, in 1907 from the lips of Gaston Cashwell, an Azusa Street pilgrim, many pastors and members of the Freewill Baptist churches spoke in tongues and led their churches into a thoroughgoing charismatic renewal. These early Baptist Pentecostals were rejected by many of their brothers in the local Baptist associations. As a result, in 1908 they organized the Pentecostal Freewill Baptist Church which today numbers about 150 churches and 13,000 members in the Central Atlantic states.[8]

Over the years since the turn of the century, former Baptists have figured largely in the formation of Pentecostal denominations. These would include C.H. Mason, founder of the Church of God in Christ, and E.N. Bell, first general superintendent of the Assemblies of God. Most of these early leaders were expelled from their churches when they testified to their Pentecostal experiences.[9]

Independent Baptist evangelists also made news in the 1950s in the heyday of the healing-deliverance crusade movement. Among those claiming Baptist ordinations were William Branham and Tommy Hicks. These men conducted some of the largest healing crusades yet seen. In 1955, Hicks preached to over 200,000 persons per night in Argentina, at that time the largest attended evangelistic crusade in all Christian history. Although nominally Baptists, these men operated in almost totally Pentecostal environments.[10]

With the advent of the neo-Pentecostal movement in the 1960s, many Baptist pastors and laymen received the baptism in the Holy Spirit and attempted to stay in their denominations. John Osteen's rejection experience was typical of the 1960s and in many quarters is still typical today.

Among the early neo-Pentecostals who faced rejection were the well-known writer Jamie Buckingham of Melbourne, Florida; Howard Conatser of Dallas, Texas; Ken Sumrall of Pensacola, Florida; and Charles Simpson of Mobile, Alabama. All of these were Southern Baptists who encountered stern opposition from their fellow pastors, in spite of solid support from their congregations.[11]

The case of Conatser became a cause celebre when his Beverly Hills Baptist Church in Dallas was rejected by the Dallas Baptist Association and the Texas Baptist state convention. Despite this situation, Beverly Hills continued to claim membership in the national Southern Baptist Convention while making every attempt to remain loyal to the denomination.

Overcoming all opposition, the Beverly Hills congregation grew to encompass over 4,000 in members in the middle 1970s. Because of its explosive growth, the church was eventually forced to conduct services in a local entertainment center known as the Bronco Bowl in order to accommodate the crowds. Opposing Conatser at this time was W.A. Criswell, pastor of the nation's largest Baptist congregation, Dallas First Baptist Church. At the height of the controversy, Criswell's own daughter received the Pentecostal experience and spoke in tongues.[12]

The Beverly Hills case was never resolved, however, since after the death of Conatser in 1978, the congregation left the Southern Baptist Convention to become an independent church. This also was the fate of the churches pastored by Simpson, Buckingham and Sumrall.

The renewal faced less opposition in the American Baptist Church (the old Northern Baptist Church, also known as the ABC), than from the Southern Baptist Church. One of the earliest neo-Pentecostals in this denomination was Howard Ervin of the Emmanuel Baptist Church in Atlantic Highlands, New Jersey. Baptized in the Holy Spirit in 1958, he soon became a proponent of Pentecostalism in the mainline churches. A graduate of Princeton Theological Seminary holding the Th.D. degree, Ervin wrote the first apology for neo-Pentecostalism in the 1967 book *These Are Not Drunken As Ye Suppose*. In later years he became a professor of theology at Oral Roberts University.[13]

Other outstanding ABC leaders were Ken Pagard of Chula Vista, California, who pioneered in organizing household groups in his church, and Gary Clark of Salem, New Hampshire. Clark's First Baptist Church grew from fewer than 100 members to over 600 before he moved to California in 1986 to pursue a ministry in world missions. For fifteen years Clark's church led all Baptist churches in New Hampshire in growth. Other early ABC charismatics were Charles Moore of Portland, Oregon, and Ray and Marjorie Bess of Du-Quoin, Illinois.[14]

During these years, Pat Robertson, a young Southern Baptist theology student at Yale University, heard about the baptism in the Holy Spirit from Robert Walker, the editor of *Christian Life* magazine. In 1957, while serving as an assistant pastor to Harald Bredesen at the Reformed Church in Mt. Vernon, New York, Robertson received the Pentecostal experience and spoke in other tongues. In 1960, Robertson returned to his native Virginia where his father had served as a Democratic U.S. senator. In 1960 he started his Christian Broadcasting Network in a broken-down studio in Portsmouth, Virginia. Since that time, Robertson's ministry has become legendary, both in American religion and in the television industry. Although still an ordained Baptist minister, he is now deeply involved in the 1988 race for the Republican nomination for president of the United States.[15]

ABC Charismatic Fellowship

The most visible group of Baptist charismatics in America are those associated with the American Baptist Church. Through the vision of laypersons Ray and Marjorie Bess, the first national conference on the Holy Spirit was conducted in 1975 at the Green Lake ABC camp in Wisconsin. Early leaders of the group were Ken Pagard and Joe Atkinson. In 1982, Gary Clark was chosen to lead the group which is now called the American Baptist Charismatic Fellowship.[16]

Outstanding ABC charismatic congregations may be found in many parts of the nation. Among them are the Bethlehem Baptist Church, Lake Oswego, Oregon, pastored by Jack Matthews; Salem Baptist Church, Salem, New Hampshire, pastored by Clement E. Sutton; First Baptist Church, Chula Vista, California, pastored by Richard Hensgen; and Redeemer Baptist Church, Monroe, Michigan, pastored by Joe Atkinson.[17]

In addition to the renewal in the United States, important charismatic growth is being evidenced in ABC mission fields around the world. Clark estimates that at least one third of all the denomination's missionaries have had a "charismatic experience."

The Southern Baptist Explosion

In recent years, there has been a veritable charismatic explosion among Southern Baptists. Although many charismatics have maintained a low profile in order to keep peace in the church, the movement has continued to grow rapidly. Despite some advances, there continue to be cases where pastors are forced to leave the denomination when their experiences become known. No one knows how many Southern Baptist pastors and missionaries have received the Pentecostal experience, but their numbers are probably very large. In the last three years, John Wimber has been instrumental in leading thousands of pastors and laypersons into the baptism in the Holy Spirit. It is also rumored that a high percentage of all Southern Baptist missionaries on the field have spoken in tongues.[18]

Several Southern Baptist ministers have also pastored independent charismatic congregations while maintaining their Southern Baptist ordinations. Two of these are Richard Hogue and Clark Whitten of Edmond, Oklahoma's Metrochurch. Hogue, who had been a popular youth evangelist during the era of the Jesus revolution in the 1960s, settled in Edmond in 1975 to begin the Metrochurch ministry. By the mid-1980s the church had grown to over 4,000 members, mostly Southern Baptists.[19]

In 1986 Whitten succeeded Hogue in the Metrochurch pastorate after a remarkable ministry at the Gateway Baptist Church of Roswell, New Mexico, where he led the Southern Baptist Convention in baptisms in 1982-83. Perhaps because Whitten and many of his members spoke in tongues, the Pecos Valley Baptist Association never received the congregation into its fellowship although the congregation remained a member in good standing in the Southern Baptist Convention.[20]

Unlike Hogue and Whitten, other Southern Baptist pastors have given up their church ordinations to follow independent ministries. One example is Larry Lea, pastor of the Church on the Rock in Rockwall, Texas. Lea, who previously served as youth minister in Conatser's Beverly Hills Church in Dallas, has seen tremendous growth in his congregation. Beginning with 13 members in 1979, his suburban congregation now numbers 11,000. In addition to the pastorate, Lea was named in 1986 to serve as dean of the theological seminary at Oral Roberts University as well as vice president of the university for spiritual affairs. His plans are to continue as pastor in Rockwall and commute weekly to his job in Tulsa.[21]

Other less well-known Southern Baptist pastors and churches continue to practice charismatic ministries. A case in point is the Friendship Baptist Church in Mansfield, Texas, pastored by LeRoy Martin. With 75 members, Friendship Baptist Church is a member of the largest Southern Baptist association in the world, the Tarrant Baptist Association. Although Martin's church is openly charismatic, he remains in good standing with the association. Some old-timers in the association have told Martin that "if the charismatics ever have to leave the association, about 40 percent of the churches will have to go."[22]

Another example is that of Don LeMaster, pastor of the West Lauderdale Baptist Church near Fort Lauderdale, Florida. Since coming to the church in 1967, LeMaster has led his church into a deepening charismatic ministry. The church does not hide its identity, since the word "charismatic" is printed on the letterhead of the church's stationary.

Although LeMaster faced some opposition from fellow Baptist pastors in the early 1970s, friendly pastors defended LeMaster's congregational right to local autonomy. In the local Gulfstream Baptist Association, "nobody bothers us," says LeMaster who has been allowed to remain as a member in good standing for over nineteen years. He ministers to a growing congregation of 3,500 members that is "growing like crazy." He plans soon to build a new sanctuary seating 2,000 persons to hold his enthusiastic crowds.[23]

The burgeoning ministry of James Robison is also a growing expression of a charismatic presence among Southern Baptists. Although he does not speak in tongues, Robison's crusades feature prayer for the sick and the exorcism of demonic spirits. He openly accepts the support of Pentecostals and speaks often in charismatic and Pentecostal circles. The support he has lost from his fellow Southern Baptists has been more than made up for by his support from Pentecostals and charismatics. His theme of restoration reflects the restorationist view of the early Pentecostals.[24]

A large group of Southern Baptists who favor a deeper spiritual life center their efforts around a magazine entitled *Fulness*. Published from Fort Worth since 1977 by editor Ras Robinson and a circle of spiritually concerned Southern Baptist friends, this periodical serves charismatic Baptists along with others outside Baptist and charismatic circles. In 1986, at least 64 percent of the readers were Baptist.[25]

Over the years, many pastors with Pentecostal roots

have also come to prominence in Southern Baptist churches. Literally hundreds of Baptist pastors were converted and received their spiritual formation in Pentecostal homes and churches. Among these are Charles Stanley, pastor of Atlanta's First Baptist Church and former president of the Southern Baptist Convention, who was born and raised in the Pentecostal Holiness Church, and Gene Garrison, pastor of the First Baptist Church in Oklahoma City, whose roots are in the Assemblies of God.

The American Baptist Church also claims as an ordained minister David Hubbard, who serves as president of Fuller Theological Seminary in Pasadena, California. Hubbard's parents were Pentecostal preachers in California.

The Future

Although American Baptist charismatics have been organized for over a decade and find open favor within the denomination, Southern Baptists have thus far been unable to organize a continuing support group. Many Spirit-filled pastors and laypersons are hoping to change this situation soon.

The New Orleans Congresses on the Holy Spirit and World Evangelization will have Baptist sessions in both 1986 and 1987. Many hope that a Southern Baptist charismatic fellowship will emerge from these congresses. LeMaster and other associates are laying plans for a charismatic fellowship for Southern Baptists similar to the American Baptist Charismatic Fellowship. This new group would be an effort to "establish lines of communication and fellowship" for Spirit-filled Southern Baptists. Their goal is "to bring spiritual renewal to the church while remaining loyal to the local, state and national conventions."[26]

It is the contention of people like C. Peter Wagner that a new "third wave" of the Spirit is breaking out in the mainline evangelical churches, including the Baptists. Studies have indicated that about twenty percent of all Baptists in America see themselves as "Pentecostal or charismatic Christians." According to a Gallup Poll taken in 1979, at least 5,000,000 U.S. Baptists feel this way. Some observers, including Wagner, estimate that today there are between 200 and 300 "fulness" congregations in the Southern Baptist Convention.[27]

Perhaps the next great wave of the Spirit will indeed take place among Southern Baptists, the nation's largest Protestant denomination. If Wagner's theory about a third wave among mainline evangelicals is correct, then a powerful outpouring of the Holy Spirit is due to fall on the Baptists in the near future.

For further information on Baptist renewal efforts, contact the following:

Gary Clark
American Baptist Charismatic Fellowship
1385 North Sierra Bonita Avenue
Pasadena, CA 91104
(818) 797-4053

Don LeMaster
Southern Baptist Charismatic Renewal
3601 Davie Boulevard
Ft. Lauderdale, FL 33312
(305) 791-8210

CHAPTER THREE

The Catholic Charismatic Renewal

On Friday evening, February 17, 1967, about thirty persons drove over the rolling hills of western Pennsylvania some thirty miles north of Pittsburgh to attend a weekend retreat in a wooden two-story inn with the name, "The Ark and the Dove." It was a brisk winter evening as they entered the hallway and began to settle in for the three-day spiritual retreat. They were literally following the motto of the house which was run by several Dutch Roman Catholic sisters: "The wilderness will lead you to your heart where I will speak" (Hos. 2:14).

Those who gathered in this wilderness retreat were professors and students from Duquesne University who formed a Bible study group known as the Chi-Rho Society. These were invited to the retreat by two Duquesne theology professors who were praying for personal spiritual renewal. They were William G. Storey and Ralph W. Keifer. Little did this group know that this meeting would be recorded in church history as the "Duquesne weekend," and that a worldwide spiritual renewal would begin in their midst before they made the drive back to Pittsburgh on Sunday.

The students had been asked to read the first four chapters of the Acts of the Apostles and David Wilkerson's book *The Cross and the Switchblade*. Only the professors had been in Pentecostal meetings before this weekend, while the students had only a hazy notion of the purpose of the gathering. The program began on Friday evening with a penance service on the theme "conviction for sin."

On Saturday, the subject turned to the book of Acts. Invited to talk that morning was Betty Shumaker, an Episcopal neo-Pentecostal who spoke simply and informally on the second chapter of Acts. As she spoke, some of the students had difficulty with the idea of hearing teaching from a Protestant, but soon her teachings on salvation brought unanticipated insights to the group.

In the early afternoon, an emergency almost brought the meeting to an end. The water pump suddenly stopped working and with no water, the leaders considered sending everyone home. Then Dave Mangan, a student, called some friends together into the chapel where they prayed for the well to be restored "in Jesus' name." After this prayer, he checked the well, and suddenly the water gushed forth. When he ran in shouting the good news, it was decided that the meeting would continue.

That night a birthday party had been planned for some of the students in the downstairs dining room. Although refreshments had been provided, no one seemed interested in gathering for the party. As Patty Gallagher went upstairs to call the students to the party, she stepped into the chapel and was overcome with a desire to pray.

Kneeling before the altar, she began to tremble under the power of God and fell to the floor. "I was flooded by the mercy and the love of God," she said.

One by one the students left the party and went upstairs to pray. The tiny room where they gathered was in reality only a bedroom converted into a chapel. It became the scene of the first Catholic charismatic prayer meeting in modern history. Miss Gallagher described for future generations the meeting in this tiny upper room:

"That night the Lord brought the whole group into the chapel...The professors then laid hands on some of the students but most of us received the baptism in the Spirit while kneeling before the blessed sacrament in prayer. Some of us started speaking in tongues; others received gifts of discernment, prophecy and wisdom."

As David Mangan entered the room, he began to weep and laugh and suddenly fell to the floor. "I was overcome with such a feeling of love that I cannot describe it," he said. On Sunday at the closing session, one student kept falling off his chair as he praised the Lord. Despite all of this glory, one of the young ladies manifested a spirit of hatred against the entire group and the manifestations of the Holy Spirit. After prayer and the laying on of hands, however, she was gloriously delivered.

Returning to the campus in Pittsburgh that evening, the excited students and professors were overwhelmed with their experiences. According to Miss Gallagher, the atmosphere was like that described in Psalm 126: "We were like men in a dream. Our mouths were filled with laughter and our lips with shouts of joy."[1]

To South Bend, East Lansing and Ann Arbor

The fire that was ignited in Pittsburgh spread quickly to other campuses where Keifer and Storey had already formed a network of friends. Letters and excited phone calls to these friends caused an air of expectancy. Even before the Duquesne weekend, Keifer and Storey had talked to Kevin Ranaghan and Bert Ghezzi and their wives in South Bend, Indiana, about the baptism in the Holy Spirit. By March 4, Storey was back in South Bend sharing his testimony with them. On March 5, Bert and Mary Lou Ghezzi, Kevin and Dorothy Ranaghan and several others received the baptism in the Holy Spirit in the Ghezzis' apartment.[2]

On March 13, a full-fledged Pentecostal renewal began in the basement of the home of Ray Bullard, a lay leader in the local chapter of the Full Gospel Business Men's Fellowship. At this meeting nine Roman Catholics received the gift of tongues, including the Ranaghans, the Ghezzis, Gerry Rauch and Jim Cavnar. Their decision to remain in the Roman Catholic Church "made the Catholic charismatic movement possible," according to Ghezzi. Also important to the future was the winning of theology professors Edward O'Connor and Josephine Massingberd Ford. Like the first Catholic Pentecostals in Pittsburgh, these young people and professors shared a deep commitment to Christ and a loyalty to their church. Their participation added youthful and prophetic fire tempered by keen intellectual insight.[3]

The same network of friends also included students and professors at Michigan State University in East Lansing and the University of Michigan in Ann Arbor. A few weeks after the Duquesne weekend, Ralph Martin and Stephen Clark, leaders in the Cursillo movement and Newman Clubs in East Lansing, Michigan, visited Pittsburgh where they were baptized in the Holy Spirit. Returning to Michigan State, they began a powerful Pentecostal movement among their student friends.[4]

Meanwhile, in South Bend, the Notre Dame Pentecostals attracted nationwide attention when campus newspapers reported on prayer meetings that took place in the administration building under the Golden Dome, a building which symbolized the university. From there the Catholic news services trumpeted the news of the "Catholic Pentecostals" at Notre Dame. Soon Catholics all over the nation and the world were aware that an unusual renewal was taking place in the American Church. The Notre Dame group eventually organized a community known as the People of Praise which was to exercise a powerful influence on the movement.[5]

Eventually Martin and Clark moved to the University of Michigan in Ann Arbor. There they sparked the organization of The Word of God community, an ecumenical group that soon grew to over 1,000 members. This community became a creative center for the movement.

By 1970, The Word of God community had become a beehive of activity where songs were composed and published and a new periodical entitled *Pastoral Newsletter* was distributed. This paper kept the leaders in touch with each other. Also, a course of instruction called the Life in the Spirit seminars was developed for those seeking to be baptized in the Holy Spirit. The weeknight charismatic prayer meeting in Ann Arbor also became the model for hundreds of similar ones that sprang up across the nation almost overnight. The early growth of the movement was highlighted in 1972 when over 20,000 copies of the *Leaders' Manual* for Life in the Spirit seminars were distributed.[6]

All over the nation the press picked up the story about the Catholic Pentecostals, as they were called in those days. To many this seemed like a contradiction in terms, yet the news had a compelling attraction that caught the imagination of the religious world.

Immediate Background

The phenomenon of Catholic Pentecostalism was not without immediate and long-term roots. The Duquesne weekend came after a year of prayer and fasting by Keifer and Storey which led them to inquire in the Pittsburgh area about people who could help them seek the baptism in the Holy Spirit. Through the help of William Lewis, a local Episcopal priest, they were directed to a home prayer meeting led by a Presbyterian neo-Pentecostal lady by the name of Florence Dodge. Early in February 1967, they attended a prayer meeting in the Dodge home where they were shocked to see a "powerful exegesis" of the book of Acts occur before their very eyes.[7]

In a short time, the two professors had been baptized in the Spirit in these prayer meetings. Strangely enough, the meetings in Flo Dodge's living room disbanded soon after the experiences with Keifer and Storey. She and her friends felt that this prayer meeting's "purpose was accomplished" after the Catholics were introduced to the Pentecostal experience.[8]

Although the outpouring of the Holy Spirit in Pittsburgh was a sovereign act of God, there were also important long-term roots to the renewal that went far beyond the Pittsburgh meetings. In retrospect, there were several renewal movements within Catholicism that were crucial to the success of the charismatic renewal when it began in 1967.

The first of these was a shift in Catholic views on the charismata that were effected in the 1800s by German theologians Adam Moehler and Matthias Scheeben. Their work led to a "revalorization of the charismata" in the modern church that ultimately bore fruit in Vatican II a century later. Also, due to the efforts of an Italian girl, Elena Guerra, Pope Leo XIII in 1897 added a novena to the Holy Spirit (a nine-day cycle of prayer between Ascension Thursday and Pentecost Sunday) to the annual prayer calendar of Catholics around the world.

Other renewal efforts such as the biblical movement, the liturgical movement and the Cursillo movement further prepared the ground for the charismatic movement to flourish in the church.

Perhaps the most important preparation for the renewal was the calling of the Second Vatican Council in Rome by Pope John XXIII in 1962. For three years, he called on Catholics around the world to pray for the bishops and the council in these words: "Lord, renew Your wonders in this our day as by a new Pentecost." Interestingly enough, the council concluded in 1965 with a positive position on the charismata which opened the church to the gifts of the Spirit in a way not seen in over 1,000 years.[9]

Early Growth and Cautious Acceptance

The early growth of the movement among Catholics was remarkable indeed. The leaders of the movement soon developed several successful approaches in organizing and leading the revival. Following the model of the Duquesne weekend, the weeknight prayer meeting developed. This became the most common gathering for the millions of Catholics who entered the movement in the years to come.

Other leaders developed covenant communities which brought the renewalists into a committed relationship designed to help those baptized in the Spirit to live out their everyday lives in a caring pastoral community. Early models were The Word of God community in Ann Arbor, the People of Praise in South Bend and the Alleluia community in Augusta, Georgia. Some of these were experiments in ecumenical relationships although there were large Catholic majorities in each one.

In 1967, a monthly meeting for a local geographical area was pioneered in Williamston, Michigan. Called a Day of Renewal, these gatherings grew in some places to number in the hundreds. In a short time, Days of Renewal became commonplace around the nation featuring a whole slate of traveling charismatic priests and laypersons serving as speakers.[10]

In that same year, the first national conference was held at Notre Dame University. With explosive early growth, these conferences were destined to attract great attention from the press and gain extensive notoriety for the movement. The first conference was held at Notre Dame in April 1967 with only eighty-five persons registered. By 1971 the conference had grown to 5,000 participants including three bishops and 230 priests. In 1972 the numbers had swelled to 11,000 participants with six bishops and 400 priests. The next year 20,000 came to Notre Dame. The highest registration came in 1976 when over 30,000 gathered in the Notre Dame football stadium to hear Cardinal Suenens speak. In this gathering were representatives from all fifty states and Canada.[11]

In 1977 the National Conference met with other Spirit-filled Christians in the ecumenical charismatic conference at Kansas City where Catholics registered fifty percent of the 52,000 participants. The largest Catholic charismatic gathering in the United States also took place in 1977 when 35,000 gathered in Atlantic City, New Jersey. These huge conferences in 1976 and 1977 represented the height of the early mushroom-like growth of the movement in the United States.[12]

To help direct this massive growth, a service committee was formed in 1970 that included six laymen and two priests. They took responsibility for directing the forming institutions of the renewal including a communications center in South Bend, the national conferences at Notre Dame, an annual leaders' conference in Ann Arbor and the *Pastoral Newsletter* which served as a clearinghouse of information for the growing network of prayer groups and conferences. In 1971 this newsletter was changed to *New Covenant* magazine which soon grew to encompass over 70,000 subscribers.

As the movement grew overseas, an international office was opened in Brussels, Belgium, at the invitation of Leon Joseph Cardinal Suenens, primate of Belgium. In 1973, Pope Paul VI had called on Suenens to serve as his international liaison to the renewal. In 1978, the international communications office was moved to Rome and placed under the direction of Tom Forrest, a missionary priest from Puerto Rico who was an early leader in the movement.[13]

The American hierarchy took early notice of the movement and issued its first statement of policy in 1969. Pointing to apparent strengths and weaknesses, the bishops recommended cautiously that the "movement be allowed to develop." This was not done without theological direction, however. Within the first five years much work had been done by such theologians as Kilian McDonnell, Edward O'Connor and Kevin Ranaghan in the area of fitting the Pentecostal experience into a Catholic framework.[14]

In a short time, books appeared explaining the movement and its teachings. These were bought by the thousands and passed from hand to hand by those hungry for a Pentecostal renewal in the church. Kevin and Dorothy Ranaghan's *Catholic Pentecostals* appeared in 1969, followed the next year by Josephine Massingberd Ford's *The Pentecostal Experience*. The first serious history of the movement, Edward O'Connor's *The Pentecostal Movement in the Catholic Church*, was published in 1971.

The task of understanding Pentecostalism was also advanced through the efforts of McDonnell and David du Plessis when in 1972 they inaugurated a dialogue between the Vatican Secretariat for the Promotion of Christian Unity and representatives of the Pentecostal churches. In essence the Catholic position on the baptism in the Holy Spirit developed by the Pentecostal Catholics was that the Holy Spirit is given at baptism, while tongues and other gifts are released or actualized later as one opens himself to the action of the Holy Spirit who already dwells within.[15]

With this understanding, the renewal moved onward toward ever greater acceptance in the church. By 1970 the movement began to be called the Catholic charismatic renewal to remove confusion arising from the earlier Catholic Pentecostal designation.

The ultimate approval of the renewal came from Pope Paul VI in 1975 at an international conference which convened in Rome. In the first-ever address from a pontiff to a charismatic gathering, the pope pointed to the positive fruit of the renewal and called it "a chance for the church and the world." To the 10,000 charismatics gathered in St. Peter's, he declared, "It will be very fortuitous for our times, for our brothers, that there should be a generation, your generation of young people, who shout out to the world the greatness of the God of Pentecost." Indeed, the Pentecostal movement had arrived in the Roman Catholic Church![16]

Period of Regionalization

After the Kansas City conference of 1977, which represented an ecumenical high-water mark for Catholics as well as Protestants, the direction of the Catholic renewal began to change course. The great national conferences gave way to many regional conferences throughout the nation. Although the movement was still growing and ever more people were participating in conferences, the public and press paid less attention than in the days when 30,000 gathered in Notre Dame.

Regionalization and the fact that Catholic Pentecostals were no longer newsworthy caused a perception that the movement had passed its peak and was going downhill after 1977. The truth was that the renewal was rapidly developing all over the world in ways not apparent to the people in America. Throughout the late 1970s and early 1980s there was significant growth in Latin America and Africa, as well as other parts of the world.

In 1984, due to a donation given by a wealthy Dutch

businessman, 7,000 priests from all over the world met in Rome for an international charismatic retreat. The pope invited them to meet in his own conference hall in the Vatican. Both Pope John Paul II and Mother Teresa addressed the conference. About 100 of those gathered there were Jesuits involved in the movement.[17]

Consolidation and Growing Pains

All renewal movements experience changes and growing pains as they develop. The Catholic charismatic movement is no exception to this rule. Through the years there have been internal differences as to the best approach to take in renewing the church. Some have believed that the parish prayer group was the best approach, while others have seen covenant communities as the most enduring avenue of change. At times, the communities themselves have not been able to agree on the best way to organize and lead the renewal.

Despite these questions, prayer groups and communities have continued to increase in the United States. In 1986, the National Service Committee estimated that there were no less than 6,500 prayer groups in the United States alone. Though some local prayer groups have seen their numbers drop from the mushroom days of the early 1970s, others have grown, while newer groups have been formed. Also, there has been a trend for prayer group members to move to larger renewal centers where they can join one of the covenant communities.[18]

In the last decade, a third center has joined Ann Arbor and South Bend as an influential hub of activity and leadership, the University of Steubenville in Ohio. Led by president Michael Scanlan, this institution has experienced remarkable growth and expansion since he first came in 1974. Today, ninety percent of the student body of 2,000 is actively involved in charismatic renewal. A fact of major importance for the future of the renewal is that Steubenville has more theology majors than Notre Dame and Catholic University combined.[19]

The editorial offices of *New Covenant* are now located in Steubenville as are also the headquarters of popular TV evangelist John Bertolucci. Every year, the university also hosts a retreat for 500 charismatic priests. Although not located in Steubenville, Mother Angelica's Eternal Word television network near Birmingham, Alabama, also provides a platform for many of the television ministries that have developed from the renewal.

The Status of the Renewal in 1986

In 1987, the Catholic charismatic renewal observed the twentieth anniversary of the Duquesne weekend. Many evaluations were made about the past and the future of the movement. It is certain, however, that in the words of Cardinal Suenens, this "surprise of the Holy Spirit" will go down in history as one of the most vigorous and influential movements in modern-day Catholicism.

Although no one knows precisely how many Catholic charismatics are in the world today, several estimates have been made which point to its enormous size. David Barrett, in his *World Christian Encyclopedia*, projected a world total of 7.5 million in 1985, while the Vatican has estimated that the total number of Catholic "glossolalics" in the world may reach a total of thirty million persons. The strength of the movement may lie somewhere between these two estimates. In any event, these figures indicate a movement of great power and magnitude.[20]

In the last several years, many prayer groups have become less ecumenical, with many becoming exclusively Roman Catholic. Because of this, some observers have perceived a re-Catholicization of the renewal, with many leaders re-emphasizing traditional Catholic positions on the Virgin Mary and the authority of the pope. One possible cause of this trend may be the increasing attacks on Catholic charismatics by some popular Pentecostal television evangelists who preach a doctrine of "come-outism."

David du Plessis has consistently pointed out that the renewal must remain both "ecumenical and charismatic" in order to flourish. By 1986, the Catholic renewal showed signs of re-establishing some of its ecumenical ties by taking a leading part in the New Orleans Congresses on the Holy Spirit and World Evangelization. The vision of a "decade of world evangelization" came from Tom Forrest, who has gained the approval of Pope John Paul II for the project.[21]

If this vision succeeds, the last decade of the twentieth century could be the greatest period of world evangelization in history. Forrest's vision is for the Christian churches of the world to present to Jesus (if He tarries) over half the population of the world on His birthday in the year 2000 A.D.

If this becomes the common goal of all the churches, then Spirit-filled Roman Catholic charismatics would shoulder a great part of the burden of converting the unbelieving populations of the world. Working with their Spirit-filled "separated brethren" in the Protestant and Pentecostal churches, they could be a major part of an army that might make the last decade of the century the greatest days in the history of the church.

For more information, write to:
  Bill Beatty
  National Service Committee
  Chariscenter USA
  P.O. Box 1065
  Notre Dame, IN 46556

CHAPTER FOUR

The Churches of Christ Renewal

In 1972 some unusual events began to occur in the venerable Belmont Church of Christ in Nashville, Tennessee. Among the first of these was a manifestation of certain spiritual gifts including speaking in tongues in a church service, a thing unthinkable in the Church of Christ tradition. Another event, which was considered even more revolutionary, came when a fifteen-year-old gospel singer by the name of Amy Grant played a guitar in the sanctuary while singing a gospel song.

These two happenings, which would not seem unusual in many churches, were among the opening volleys in a revolution that is affecting hundreds of congregations in the Church of Christ-Christian Church-Disciples of Christ tradition. The pastor of the century-old congregation was Don Finto, a soft-spoken former professor at David Lipscomb College, an intellectual center of the Church of Christ.[1]

The story of the renewal in this church is one of the more remarkable ones in recent history in light of the hard line taken by the Church of Christ against both glossolalia and instrumental music throughout its history. In the twentieth century, the Churches of Christ have felt a special zeal to engage Pentecostals in public debates since both traditions claim to have uncovered original New Testament Christianity.

The Campbell-Stone Tradition

To understand the revolutionary impact of these events at the Belmont Church, one must understand the theology and history of the restoration tradition which produced the congregation. The two founders of the movement were Alexander Campbell and Barton Stone, both ministers on the American frontier who desired to promote the unity of the churches. Stone, an ordained Presbyterian minister from Kentucky, and Campbell, son of a Presbyterian preacher in Pennsylvania, were primarily concerned with the creeds and sectarian nature of American denominationalism.[2]

Stone was pastor of the Presbyterian congregation in Cane Ridge, Kentucky, when the Second Great Awakening began in the area in 1801. Cane Ridge became famous for the frontier demonstrations which included shouting, spiritual dancing, the "holy laugh," the "singing exercise" and being "slain in the Spirit." Stone was greatly impressed with the depth as well as the fervor of the revival. In his *Autobiography* written in 1847, Stone described some of the scenes at Cane Ridge, now considered the mother church of the restorationist tradition:

> The scene to me was strange. It baffled description. Many, very many fell down, as men slain in battle, and continued for hours together in an apparently breathless and motionless state....After

lying thus for hours, they obtained deliverance. The gloomy cloud, which had covered their faces, seemed gradually and visibly to disappear, and hope in smiles brightened into joy—they would rise shouting deliverance, and then would address the surrounding multitude in language truly eloquent and impressive.

Of all the phenomena at Cane Ridge, Stone was most impressed with the "singing exercise" whereby the saints "in a very happy state of mind would sing most melodiously, not from the mouth or nose, but entirely in the breast...it was most heavenly. None could ever be tired of hearing it," said Pastor Stone.

In the end, Stone pronounced that these "exercises" were not of Satan, but of God. "After attending to many such cases, my conviction was complete that it was a good work—the work of God; nor has my mind wavered since on the subject." He further stated that "the devil has always tried to ape the works of God, to bring them into disrepute. But that cannot be a satanic work, which brings men to humble confession and forsaking of sin—to solemn prayer—fervent praise and thanksgiving, and to sincere and affectionate exhortations to sinners to repent and go to Jesus the saviour."[3]

After the high days at Cane Ridge subsided, Stone led a New Light movement in 1804 which called for Christian unity through the recognition of autonomous congregations. He wanted his followers to be known simply as Christians.

A few years later, Alexander Campbell led a similar movement in western Pennsylvania where he emphasized believer's baptism by immersion. Joining at first with the Baptists, Campbell edited a periodical called the *Millennial Harbinger*. By 1830, however, Campbell and his followers parted company with the Baptists because of several disagreements. His followers then began to call themselves Disciples.[4]

In 1832, Stone and Campbell joined forces in forming the movement which today carries the names Christian Churches (Disciples of Christ), Churches of Christ and the Christian Churches/Churches of Christ. In the early years, and even today, the followers of Stone and Campbell were popularly called Campbellites.[5]

Campbell's teachings were gathered in a book titled *The Christian System*, published in 1835. Other major teachings of the movement were systematized by Walter Scott, a colleague of Campbell, who developed a plan of salvation based on objective positive steps into the church. They included faith, repentance, baptism, remission of sins, and the gift of the Holy Spirit. Disciples were also known for observing the Lord's supper every Sunday, in contrast to most Protestant groups who practiced a monthly or quarterly observance.[6]

Church fathers also refused to organize any central structures since they saw the local congregation as the highest authority seen in the *New Testament*. In general, Campbell and his followers rejected all creeds and speculative theology as tests of fellowship since they were "manmade." The New Testament was taken to be the ultimate rule of faith and practice.

Although these churches remained united during the Civil War, they suffered divisions in the twentieth century over theological differences. During the last decades of the nineteenth century, a large number of conservative Southern congregations began to teach a formula of biblical interpretation which states: "Where the Bible speaks, we speak, but where the Bible is silent, we are silent.'' Above all, emphasis was placed on avoiding matters where the Scriptures were silent. Among other things, these churches forbade musical instruments in worship and taught that anyone not baptized in a Church of Christ congregation could not be a true Christian. More and more, these congregations referred to themselves as Churches of Christ.[7]

In 1906, the federal census listed these churches separately under the name Churches of Christ, with the other Christian Churches listed as Disciples of Christ. The ministers also were listed in separate books during this period. After this separation, the Disciples of Christ became known as one of the most liberal Protestant denominations in America, while the Churches of Christ gained a reputation as one of the most conservative church bodies. The fiery evangelism of the Churches of Christ soon led to such growth that this body surpassed the other in size.[8]

By the early 1950s, a large number of congregations that did not feel at home in either one of the foregoing groups formed a third group known as the Christian Churches/Churches of Christ. Most of these churches departed from the Disciples of Christ over what they saw as liberal tendencies in the church. Altogether, these are the churches that prefer to be called ''restoration churches'' because they see themselves as attempting to restore New Testament Christianity in the modern world.[9]

Altogether they form one of the largest religious movements to have originated in America. By 1985 their combined membership in the United States had reached about five million. The largest of these, the non-instrumental Churches of Christ claimed 2.5 million members. [10]

Pat Boone and Don Finto

The first well-known Church of Christ member to receive the Pentecostal experience was the entertainer Pat Boone. Already famous for his Church of Christ testimony, Boone was as well-known as a crusader for his church as he was for his white shoes. In 1968 he met George Otis who told him about the baptism in the Holy Spirit. Soon Boone and his wife, Shirley (the daughter of country entertainer Red Foley), and their four daughters not only were speaking in tongues but were leading others into the experience while baptizing new converts in the Boones' swimming pool.

Because of this, Boone was excommunicated from his Church of Christ congregation and in time joined Jack Hayford's Foursquare Church on the Way in Van Nuys, California. The story of Boone's experiences were given in his 1970 autobiography entitled *A New Song*. [11]

In 1969, Don Finto had a similar experience in the Holy Spirit while serving as head of the foreign languages department at David Lipscomb College. Because he disagreed with the stand of his church, Finto in 1971 resigned his position in the college and his pastorate of a local Church of Christ near Nashville. [12]

He was then offered the pastorate of the Belmont Church, at that time a declining downtown congregation with only seventy members. Although the elders had heard of his experience with the Holy Spirit, they nevertheless asked him to take the church. After the advent of the gifts of the Spirit and instrumental music in the church, all of the original elders resigned but one. Finto then inaugurated new church ministries to drug addicts, using country and Christian musicians, and to street people in a coffee house ministry. After this, the church grew by leaps and bounds.[13]

By 1985 the Belmont congregation had grown to over 2,000 members and, because of its burgeoning attendance, was forced to conduct its Sunday worship services in a local junior high school in order to accommodate the crowds who could no longer squeeze into the old sanctuary. Many members of the Nashville music community began to attend the church which is now famous for its music. In addition to Amy Grant, the Belmont Church is home to such Nashville musicians as Michael W. Smith, Billy Sprague, Kathy Troccoli, Marty McCall and the Slaughters.[14]

Conference on Spiritual Renewal

The leader in organizing the renewal in the restorationist tradition is Jim Bevis from Nashville, who was born, raised and educated in the Church of Christ. Bevis, who was ordained in 1974, enjoyed successful pastorates in Atlanta and Houston after serving for several years as a Christian education director and campus minister in America's largest Church of Christ in Lubbock, Texas.[15]

In 1975, while pastoring the Brook Valley Church of Christ in Atlanta, Bevis hungered for a deeper walk with God. Through the ministry of Tim Ruthven of New Zealand, he received the baptism in the Holy Spirit and spoke in tongues. His congregation "suffered no adverse effects" when he introduced mildly charismatic worship in the services.[16]

While pastoring the Brook Valley Church, he searched for others in his tradition who had also experienced the moving of the Holy Spirit including the gifts of the Spirit. In 1977 and early 1978, he found fifteen men in the Churches of Christ and Disciples of Christ whom he referred to as "renewed brothers." In January 1978, these men met in St. Louis for the first gathering which was later to be known as the Conference on Spiritual Renewal. Here Robert Yawberg and Wayne Fife of Fort Wayne, Indiana, excitedly told the group about the Kansas City Conference of 1977.[17]

In 1980, the first national Conference on Spiritual Renewal convened at the Disciples of Christ Historical Society in Nashville, where the group sought the Lord together, shared their lives and re-examined the various works and gifts of the Holy Spirit as manifested at Cane Ridge. This dimension of revivalism they saw as part of the heritage of their tradition.

Subsequent meetings have been held in Nashville hosted by the Belmont Church which is considered the flagship congregation of the renewal movement among restoration churches. Those constituting the board of the conference include Bevis, Finto and Yawberg; Tom Smith of Cincinnati; Deering Manning of Jacksonville, Florida; Jack Haun of Indianapolis; Grant Edwards of Springfield, Ohio; Gerald Denny of Urbana, Illinois; LaVerne Campbell of Atlanta; Worth Gibson of Jonesboro, Arkansas; Ogle Hall of Nashville; Sid Woodruff of Atlanta; and Bob Bethke of Dallas.[18]

Although the conference does not specifically identify itself as charismatic, most of its members are supporters of the present-day move of the Holy Spirit. Charismatic and non-charismatic participants are welcomed and made to feel at home. Since 1980 the CSR has conducted seven renewal conferences. During this time over 2,500 have registered for these meetings representing over 500 congregations and pastors. According to Bevis, the conference has become "an oasis where exhausted believers and churches come for renewed life."[19]

Other ministries include regional conferences throughout the nation in addition to the annual national conference in Nashville. The group also publishes a quarterly periodical called *Paraclete Journal* which keeps members in touch with the movement and with what God is doing throughout the body of Christ.[20]

Outstanding congregations that have experienced renewal in recent years include the Belmont Church, Nashville, Tennessee, Don Finto, pastor; Broadway Christian Church, Fort Wayne, Indiana, Bob Yawberg, pastor; Fellowship Christian Church, Cincinnati, Ohio, Tom Smith, pastor; Orange Park Christian Church, Jacksonville, Florida, T.D. Manning, pastor; and House Christian Fellowship in Springfield, Ohio.

There is an air of excitement and expectation among these leaders. Many feel that the movement lost its most critical spiritual dynamic after the waning of the Cane Ridge awakening which gave the church its birth. "I am convinced that Pentecostal power coupled with the prevailing Word of God will bring alive the restoration churches today," Bevis says. "There is a stirring going on in our movement. It is the fresh breath of the Holy Spirit. Thousands are hungering and thirsting for more. Many are coming to the Fountain of Living Water. We are on the edge of a great spiritual breakthrough among restoration churches."

For further information, write to:

THE 20TH-CENTURY PENTECOSTAL EXPLOSION

Jim Bevis
Conference on Spiritual Renewal
P.O. Box 40325
Nashville, TN 37204
(615) 385-2904

CHAPTER FIVE

The Churches of God

Of the 200 or so denominations in the United States with a variation of the name Church of God, the largest one is a Pentecostal body with headquarters in Cleveland, Tennessee. Because of the many churches with similar names, the major bodies with the name Church of God have added headquarters designations to distinguish them from sister churches. Other ones such as the Church of God (Anderson, Indiana) sometimes also add the byline "non-Pentecostal" to avoid confusion with the Pentecostals who also boast of a denomination known as the Pentecostal Church of God.

In addition to this, there are at least three denominations headquartered in the small city of Cleveland, Tennessee, with the name Church of God: the Church of God (Cleveland, Tennessee), the Church of God of Prophecy and the Jerusalem Acres Church of God. Another related group with headquarters in Huntsville, Alabama, carries the name Church of God, World Headquarters. None of these churches is related to the Winebrenner Church of God which antedates most of the above mentioned groups.

In August 1986, the Church of God (Cleveland, Tennessee) observed a centennial harking back to what is claimed as the beginning of the Pentecostal movement in the United States. Over 35,000 persons gathered in Atlanta for the 61st General Assembly, the largest gathering in the history of the church.

The Christian Union

What was commemorated was a meeting in 1886 at Barney Creek in Monroe County, Tennessee, under the leadership of R.G. Spurling Sr., where a group known as the Christian Union was formed. Spurling, a Baptist, called for a new reformation in the church since, by his reckoning, all the other churches had fallen into a spiritual dark age.[1]

After some years, new groups appeared around the countryside. Church of God historians such as Charles W. Conn point to the revival in the Schearer Schoolhouse in the Cokercreek community of North Carolina as an important root of the church. During a revival in 1896 conducted by evangelists, William Martin, Milton McNabb and Joe M. Tipton, some unusual phenomena electrified the community.

This meeting exhibited the doctrines and usages of the fire-baptized movement which was spreading rapidly at the time. Such fanaticisms as third, fourth and fifth baptisms of fire, dynamite and oxidite were taught to the faithful who were also forbidden to eat pork, drink coffee or violate any of the dietary laws of the Old Testament.

Because of these extremes, rowdies descended on the meetings and violence was visited upon the hapless worshippers. It was also reported that some of the people at the Schearer Schoolhouse spoke in strange tongues when they received the baptism of fire. After the excitement of the revival died away, Tipton, Martin, McNabb and R.G. Spurling Jr. continued to preach in whatever schoolhouses and brush arbors they could secure, despite the persecution and rejection of their mountaineer neighbors.²

A.J. Tomlinson

The Christian Union was reorganized as the Holiness Church at Camp Creek in Western North Carolina on May 15, 1902, in the home of lay preacher W.F. Bryant. The pastor of the church at this time was R.G. Spurling Jr. This church might have existed alone except for the visit in 1903 of a traveling Bible salesman from Indiana by the name of Ambrose Jessup Tomlinson. A Quaker, Tomlinson was in the holiness wing of Quakerism and earned a living as a colporteur by selling Bibles and other religious materials to the pious mountain folk of eastern Tennessee and western North Carolina.³

In the summer of 1903, Tomlinson, who had visited the region occasionally since 1896, happened upon the tiny congregation at Camp Creek and was invited to join. His education and knowledge of the Bible were obviously superior to that of the congregation, and so he was looked on as a prize that could help the struggling group. Before joining, however, Tomlinson spent the night in "prevailing prayer" on nearby Burger Mountain where he received a vision of the Church of God of the last days which would restore the entire body of Christ to the faith of the New Testament.⁴

The next day, June 13, 1903, the Hoosier salesman joined the church with the understanding that it was the Church of God of the Bible and not a man-made organization. With the winning of Tomlinson, the Camp Creek Church gained one of the great organizing geniuses of modern American church history.[5]

In a short time, Tomlinson had planted churches in Union Grove and Drygo in Tennessee and a small congregation in Jones, Georgia. A mission was also established in nearby Cleveland which became a center of activities for the group. By 1906 these churches were able to call the first general gathering to consider matters of common interest. Thus on January 26 and 27, 1906, the first general assembly convened in the home of J.C. Murphy of Camp Creek, North Carolina.[6]

Since Tomlinson was serving as pastor of the local church, he was selected to serve as the moderator. The new church adopted strict teachings of personal holiness which forbade their members to use tobacco or alcohol. Foot washing as a required ordinance was approved as was the use of Sunday schools. To avoid the errors of denominationalism, Tomlinson wrote into the record that none of the *Minutes* should ever be used "to establish a sect or denomination." The congregations represented by the twenty-one delegates who gathered in the living room of the Murphy home were to be known simply as Holiness churches.[7]

In the second meeting which convened in Bradley County, Tennessee, in January 1907, the group chose the name Church of God since it was a name mentioned in the Bible. There seemed to be no connection with any other church in America other than Tomlinson's knowledge of the Church of God (Anderson, Indiana) and the Winebrenner group in Pennsylvania.

The new denomination was typical of the Holiness churches formed in America in this period. The second blessing of entire sanctification was sought as a baptism with the Holy Ghost which freed the seeker from the results of original sin. Also strongly affirmed was the certainty of divine healing for the body in answer to prayer. The fanaticisms of 1896 gave way to a more moderate but still radical version of the American holiness movement. Under Tomlinson's dynamic leadership, the Church of God planted churches throughout the mountain areas of Tennessee, Georgia, Kentucky, West Virginia and North Carolina.

Pentecost

In 1906, Tomlinson and other leaders of the church heard the news from Azusa Street about a new Pentecost characterized by speaking in other tongues. The news was welcomed in the environs of Cleveland as another wave of holiness revival which could bless all the churches. Tomlinson was especially interested in the new doctrine and experience. In his diary, he recorded every conceivable spiritual manifestation he saw in his meetings, but never had he recorded a case of glossolalia.[8]

With extreme interest, he visited Birmingham, Alabama, in June 1907 to hear Gaston Barnabas Cashwell, a North Carolina preacher from the Pentecostal Holiness Church, who had received the baptism at Azusa Street. Cashwell was on a whirlwind tour of the South explaining the Pentecostal movement to the large crowds of Holiness people who gathered to hear the new tongues. Although Tomlinson missed meeting Cashwell, he did meet with M.M. Pinson, a later founding father of the Assemblies of God, and talked with him about the new Pentecostal movement. Although Tomlinson did not receive the tongues experience in

Birmingham in 1907, he returned to Cleveland determined that his church would enter into this new spiritual experience.

Calling on the church to pray for a new Pentecost, the general moderator invited Cashwell to preach in the following general assembly which convened in January 1908 in Cleveland. By the time Cashwell arrived, which was after the general assembly officially closed, many of the pastors had already received the baptism and were speaking with other tongues. They were now praying for their leader.[9]

Tomlinson's baptism was one of the most colorful in all the literature of Pentecostalism. While Cashwell was preaching, the general overseer fell to the floor behind the pulpit with his head under a chair. He then spoke in not one, but ten different tongues in succession. With this event, it was a foregone conclusion that the Church of God would be a part of the growing Pentecostal movement. After January 1907, glossolalia appeared in practically every service that Tomlinson observed in the churches. Tongues, interpretations and prophecies became so prevalent that major decisions of the general assemblies were taken in accordance with charismatic directions brought forth by tongues and interpretations.[10]

The new dynamic brought on by the Pentecostal experience caused fantastic growth in the fledgling church. Almost all of north Cleveland was won to the church by 1909. Communities all over the South were soon visited by itinerant preachers who ministered in mill villages, mining camps, towns, crossroads and larger cities in the region. In time, the churches followed their migrant members north into the industrial cities of the

Northeast and the Midwest. The Church of God indeed began to move like a mighty army across the land. In 1910 some 1,005 members were reported in twenty-seven churches. By 1920 those figures had mushroomed to 14,606 members in 389 congregations.[11]

Divisions

The impetus of these early years was broken, however, after World War I when questions arose over the methods Tomlinson used in running the church. Over the years, he had gathered more power into his own hands and had even led the church in adopting a new constitution in 1914 giving him the overseer's position for life. In 1917 an openly theocratic constitution was adopted, confirming his lifetime appointment. By 1922 dissatisfaction arose over the alleged mishandling of monies. A struggle ensued in the following months between Tomlinson and a council of elders led by Flavius Josephus Lee and J.S. Llewellyn.[12]

In a church trial which took place in Bradley County, Tennessee, in 1923, the council of elders removed Tomlinson from his office, whereupon he withdrew from the church. He and his followers then organized another denomination as the Church of God. With monies arriving by mail in Cleveland, the post office was at a loss as to how the mail should be delivered. This led to a protracted lawsuit which eventually was decided by the Supreme Court of Tennessee. The final decision resulted in the churches being legally known as the Church of God and the Tomlinson Church of God.[13]

The Church of God of Prophecy

This situation with the Tomlinson Church of God continued until Tomlinson's death in 1943 when a question of future leadership opened between the followers of Tomlinson's two sons, Homer and Milton. Homer, a longtime preacher, had considered himself heir to his father's position. Many pastors, however, felt that Homer was unstable and preferred the younger son Milton, who had worked as a printer in the White Wing publishing house owned by the church and as a pastor in Kentucky. When Milton was chosen overseer, Homer left to organize yet another denomination known as the Church of God, World Headquarters. Until his death in 1968, his headquarters were in Queens, New York. Over the years he became famous worldwide for his claims of being the king and bishop of the entire world.[14]

The church Milton headed adopted the name Church of God of Prophecy in 1952 and pursued a vigorous ministry from a modern headquarters in Cleveland. Both the World Headquarters churches and Church of God of Prophecy continued to teach Tomlinson's eschatological vision of a day when all churches would flow into the Church of God that the founder had envisioned on Burger Mountain in 1903.

Church of God (Cleveland, Tennessee)

The Church of God, led after 1923 by F.J. Lee, eventually became known as the Church of God (Cleveland, Tennessee) for reasons of identity and became the mainstream of the movement. By 1943, it had joined the National Association of Evangelicals and later was a charter member in the formation of the Pentecostal Fellowship of North America in 1948. It also became one of the largest and fastest-growing Pentecostal churches in the world. Early missions efforts made the Churches of God a dominant force in the Caribbean

nations. Later mergers established strong affiliations
with national churches in South Africa, Indonesia and
Romania.[15]

In 1985, the Cleveland Church of God numbered
1,606,177 members and adherents in over eighty nations of the world. In the United States, 5,536 churches
ministered to a membership of 532,502 members. In
the United States alone the church counts a ministerium
of 11,611 licensed and ordained men and women.[16]

The largest and best-known Church of God (Cleveland, Tennessee) congregation in America is the Mount
Paran Church of God in Atlanta pastored by Paul Lavern
Walker. This dynamic congregation has grown to over
5,000 members under Walker's leadership. Since 1910
the *Church of God Evangel* has chronicled the growth
and activities of the church. The present general overseer
is Raymond E. Crowley who administers the denomination from a modern headquarters edifice in Cleveland.

The Church of God of Prophecy has also grown in
America and around the world. In 1985 the American
church counted 73,952 members with 153,048 members
on the mission fields. Church activities are controlled
by the general assembly which each year attracts 20,000
people to the headquarters complex in Cleveland. Now
in his eightieth year, Milton Tomlinson celebrated forty-
three years of leading the church in the 1986 General
Assembly.[17]

For further information contact:
  Lewis J. Willis
  Office of Public Relations
  The Church of God (Cleveland, TN)
  Keith and 25th

Cleveland, TN 37311
(615) 472-3361

Perry Gillum
The Church of God of Prophecy
Bible Place
Cleveland, TN 37311
(615) 479-8511

CHAPTER SIX

The Church of God in Christ

It is commonly thought that the Assemblies of God constitutes the largest Pentecostal denomination in the United States. It is also commonly thought that the oldest Pentecostal denomination in the nation is the Church of God headquartered in Cleveland, Tennessee. It just may be, however, that the nation's largest and oldest Pentecostal group is neither of the above, but the largely black church known as the Church of God in Christ with headquarters in Memphis, Tennessee.

Chartered in 1897, the Church of God in Christ is unquestionably the first legally chartered body among the American Pentecostal denominations. With a claimed membership that exceeds three million persons, this church is twice the size of the Assemblies of God in the United States. Though some would debate these claims, the church is clearly one of the oldest and largest of all the Pentecostal movements in the world—and also one of the fastest-growing.[1]

C.H. Mason and C.P. Jones

The roots of the Church of God in Christ lie deep in

the late nineteenth-century Holiness movement in the Southern states. These roots are also grounded in the culture and history of the American blacks. The story of this church in its early years was also largely the biographies of two prominent church leaders: C.P. Jones and C.H. Mason.

Charles Harrison Mason, born in 1866 in Bartlett, Tennessee, was the son of former slaves. He grew up in a Missionary Baptist Church and as a young man felt the call to preach. In 1893 he entered Arkansas Baptist College to study for the ministry but was soon grieved by the liberal teachings he heard. He left school after only three months because he felt that there was "no salvation in the schools or colleges." In 1895, while on a visit to Jackson, Mississippi, he met Charles Price Jones, another young Baptist preacher, who was to affect his life greatly and was then serving as pastor of the Mt. Helms Baptist Church of Jackson, Mississippi.[2]

Later that year, Jones and Mason traveled to Lexington, Mississippi, where they preached the Wesleyan doctrine of entire sanctification as a second work of grace. Initiating Holiness revivals in local Baptist churches, the two fiery preachers were soon disfellowshipped and forbidden to preach in the churches of the local Baptist associations. They thereupon opened an historic revival campaign in a cotton gin in Lexington in February 1896 and saw the first local congregation formed.[3]

The name for the new group came to Mason in March 1897 while walking the streets of Little Rock, Arkansas. The Church of God in Christ seemed to be a biblical name for the new Holiness church in Lexington. The teachings of the new group were the typical perfectionistic doctrines of the turn-of-the-century Holiness movement. Those receiving the sanctification experience were thenceforth holy and known as saints. These Holiness people neither smoked tobacco nor drank alcohol. They dressed modestly, worked hard and paid their bills. They praised the Lord fervently with shouting and spiritual dancing. Among them the poorest share-cropper could become a preacher of the gospel and even become a bishop in the church.[4]

In 1897, the Church of God in Christ was legally chartered in nearby Memphis, Tennessee, the first Pentecostal church in America to obtain such recognition. After this, Memphis became the headquarters of the church and the site of the annual convocations which became huge rallying gathcrings for the faithful.[5]

The church continued peacefully for several years with dual leadership. Though Jones was the leader of the church, Mason was the dominant personality. They were a fine and harmonious team. Mason was known for his godly character and preaching ability, while Jones was known for his hymns, many of which became popular throughout the nation. Two of his better known hymns were "Deeper, Deeper" and "Come Unto Me."

Pentecost Comes to Memphis

The tranquility between Mason and Jones was broken, however, when in 1906 word reached Memphis of the new Pentecost being experienced in Los Angeles in a little mission on Azusa Street. The pastor of the mission was a black man, William J. Seymour, who preached that the saints, although sanctified, had not received the baptism in the Holy Ghost until they had spoken in tongues as the initial evidence. It was said that all the gifts of the Spirit were being restored to the church at Azusa Street and that white people were coming to be taught by blacks and to worship together in apparent equality.[6]

The news from Azusa Street met with a divided response in the Church of God in Christ which by now had spread widely into Tennessee, Mississippi and Arkansas. Jones was cool to the new teaching, while Mason was eager to travel to Los Angeles to investigate the revival. Mason for years had claimed that God endowed him with supernatural characteristics, which were manifested in dreams and visions. In the end, Mason prevailed on two fellow leaders to accompany him on a pilgrimage to Azusa Street. In March 1907, Mason, along with J.A. Jeter and D.J. Young, traveled to Los Angeles.

What they saw at Azusa Street was powerful and convincing. In the words of Frank Bartleman, "the color line was washed away by the blood." People of all races and nationalities worshipped together in striking unity and equality. The gift of tongues was matched by other gifts such as interpretation, healing, words of knowledge and wisdom, and exorcism of demons. In a short time, Mason and Young received the baptism, spoke in tongues and returned to Memphis eager to share their new experience with the rest of the church.

When they arrived, they were surprised to find that another Azusa Street pilgrim, Glen A. Cook, a white man, had already visited the church and preached the new Pentecostal doctrine. Many of the saints had accepted the message and were speaking in tongues as the Spirit gave them utterance. Everyone did not accept Cook's message, however, chief of whom was C.P. Jones who in 1907 was serving as the general overseer and presiding elder of the denomination.[7]

A struggle for the future of the church ensued as the new Pentecostal party led by Mason vied with Jones for the leadership of the church. By August 1907 the issue came to a head in the general assembly of the church which met in Jackson, Mississippi. After a very lengthy discussion which lasted three days and into the nights, the assembly withdrew the right hand of fellowship from C.H. Mason and all who promulgated the doctrine of speaking with tongues "as the initial evidence." When Mason left the assembly, about half of the ministers and laity left with him.

In September 1907, the Pentecostal group gathered another convocation in Memphis where the Church of God in Christ became a full-fledged member of the Pentecostal movement. In 1909, after two years of struggle, the courts allowed the Mason faction to retain the name Church of God in Christ and a Pentecostal statement was added to the articles of faith which separated the baptism in the Holy Spirit from the experience of Sanctification. It stated that "the full baptism in the Holy Spirit is evidenced by speaking in other tongues."

Although tongues were thus welcomed and accepted in the church, other manifestations of the Spirit's presence were also commonly seen as evidence of the indwelling Holy Spirit, such as healing, prophecy, shouting and "dancing in the Spirit."

After 1907, a lengthy legal struggle ensued over who could use the name and charter of the Church of God in Christ—the followers of Mason or the followers of Jones. The issue was finally settled in the courts of Shelby County, Tennessee, when, in 1909, the court awarded victory to Mason and his Pentecostal party.

They therefore continued to use the name and charter of the Church of God in Christ, while Jones and his non-Pentecostal followers separated to form a new group which they named the Church of Christ (Holiness) U.S.A.[8]

Growth and Divisions

From its base in Memphis, the Church of God in Christ spread rapidly over the United States. Its first base was in the South where the Pentecostal revival swept through many black neighborhoods like a prairie fire. Mason often organized churches by preaching in the streets. As the Pentecostal movement spread among whites in the South, Mason occasionally visited these churches and was recognized as the outstanding leader among the black Pentecostals. In 1921 in New Jersey, he met again with William J. Seymour where the two black Pentecostal apostles talked about the old Azusa days. Although the two leaders were not in the same denomination, they remained lifelong friends.

As his church grew, Mason demonstrated his organizing genius. Each diocese was led by a bishop who usually served for life. Jurisdictions were divided and subdivided as the church grew so that the church spread into all of the states of the Union by the end of World War II. The church was and remained episcopal in government with great power exercised by the bishops. From 1910 to 1916, Mason began four major departments that aided in the growth of the church. They were the women's department, the Sunday school, the Young People's Willing Workers (YPWW), and the home and foreign missions department.[9]

The basic teachings of the church were also defined in the early years. Basically a Holiness church, the denomination continued to teach an experience and life of holiness as the ultimate goal of the Christian life. To this was added the Pentecostal baptism with the Holy Spirit which brought into the life of the church and the believers all the gifts of the Spirit. When the "oneness" controversy erupted in the Pentecostal world after 1913, the Church of God in Christ remained staunchly trinitarian. Added to the sacraments of water baptism and the Lord's supper was the ordinance of foot washing.

An important early teaching of the church was pacifism, or the teaching that Christians should not engage in war. Because of his determined stand on this issue, Mason was jailed in 1918 in Lexington, Mississippi, because he forbade his followers to serve in the armed forces of the nation. While he was imprisoned, a storm blew the roof off the courthouse building, whereupon the magistrates released him the next day.

Throughout his life, Mason was hounded for his pacifist views, even to the point that the FBI kept a file on his activities. Like most of the other Pentecostal bodies in the United States, however, the Church of God in Christ softened this stand during World War II because of the apparent evils of fascism and Naziism.[10]

The "Gentleman's Agreement"

Mason never accepted the separation of Christians on the basis of race. Although he never openly fought the Jim Crow system of racial segregation, he felt keenly the racial separations among Pentecostals that came after the halcyon days of Azusa Street. Indeed, for many years Mason's church was the most integrated denomination in the United States. In the most racist period of American history (1890-1924), the Pentecostals stood out as a glaring exception to the segregation of the times.[11]

In fact, hundreds of white Pentecostal preachers were ordained at Mason's hands and were given ministerial credentials from the Church of God in Christ in the years before World War I. One reason for this situation was that the Church of God in Christ was the only incorporated Pentecostal denomination in the nation for many years. In order for a minister to be bonded for performing marriages, to be deferred from the draft, or to obtain clergy permits on the railroads, he had to demonstrate that he was a minister of a recognized religious body. Mason's church had the prized incorporation charter which made it attractive for hundreds of white ministers to join his church. Beyond this, however, Mason's powerful preaching, charismatic personality and brotherly love, despite segregation, attracted thousands of whites.

As time went on, some of the white pastors began to hold separate Bible conferences while keeping their relationship with Mason intact. Finally a "gentleman's agreement" was struck whereby the whites could issue credentials in Mason's name and that of the Church of God in Christ, the only stipulation being that no credentials would be given to anyone who was unworthy.

Just before the beginning of World War I, a large group of white Pentecostal ministers became dissatisfied with this arrangement and began organizing a new denomination which could also be chartered, thus granting the above benefits to the ministers of the new group. Most of the founders of the Assemblies of God who gathered in Hot Springs, Arkansas, in April 1914 carried credentials with the Church of God in Christ.

Although Mason and his group were nominally invited to attend the Hot Springs conclave, no letters of invitation were sent to the black ministers.

Mason did attend the meeting, however, and was invited to preach on the Thursday night of the convention. His choir sang a special number after which the venerable bishop preached a sermon on the wonders of God as seen in the lowly sweet potato. Despite Mason's appearance, the Assemblies of God organized a largely white denomination which soon became the largest Pentecostal church in the country. Thus the organization of the Assemblies of God was at least partially a racial separation from Mason's church.[12]

After 1914, the leaders of the white Pentecostal denominations looked on the Church of God in Christ as the black Pentecostal movement for the United States. Black converts in white churches were encouraged to join the Church of God in Christ in the light of the segregation practiced at the time.[13]

Some of the church's greatest growth came in the years following World Wars I and II when blacks migrated en masse to the large industrial cities of the North. Millions of Southern blacks moved to New York City, Detroit, Philadelphia, Chicago, Boston, Los Angeles and other urban centers to escape the agrarian poverty that still blighted much of the South.

These migrants brought their churches with them to the cities where they settled. Many of these were members of the Church of God in Christ. Often they settled in storefront buildings or bought the elegant church buildings sold by whites who fled the inner cities for the suburbs.

The Pentecostal churches proved to be the most

successful in serving this mass of humanity which crowded into the urban ghettos. In some cities almost every block boasted a Church of God in Christ; in many cases humble and unostentatious, but nevertheless a powerfully redemptive force in the neighborhood. The story of one of these urban migrant churches was power-fully portrayed in James Baldwin's book *Go Tell It on the Mountain*, which was an autobiographical account of his childhood in a storefront Pentecostal church in Harlem. Because of this massive migration and the un-questioned attraction of Pentecostal worship for the disinherited blacks, both rural and urban, the Church of God in Christ experienced massive growth in the mid-dle of the century.[14]

At the time of Mason's death in 1961, his church had entered every state in the Union and numbered some 400,000 members in the United States. This compared favorably with the record of John Wesley who counted 100,000 Methodist followers when he died in 1791. Before his death, Mason had constructed the massive Mason Temple in Memphis where the faithful gathered annually for the great convocations which became the largest annual gatherings in the city of Memphis. This temple, which seats almost 10,000, was unable to hold the convocation crowds which annually numbered some 40,000 persons. When he died in 1961 at the age of 95, the church was given permission to bury Mason in the lobby of the temple, the only person so honored in the history of the city.[15]

After Mason's death a power struggle ensued over who would inherit the mantle of the fallen apostle. The temporary winner was O.T. Jones Sr., who served as senior bishop from 1962 to 1968. But in the end, it was

Mason's son-in-law, J.O. Patterson, who became the heir to Mason's legacy. Elected to lead the church in November of 1968, Patterson was given the title of presiding bishop. He has since led the church to its greatest growth and development. Despite a schism in 1969 in which fourteen Church of God in Christ bishops formed the Church of God in Christ, International (now claiming 200,000 members), the church has continued to grow rapidly.[16]

In 1964 a census was taken of the church in the United States and the membership was reported at 425,000 members in 4,100 congregations. The next census was not attempted until 1982. As a result of that count, the *Yearbook of American and Canadian Churches* reported an American membership for the church at 3,709,861 persons in 9,982 congregations. This is one of the most explosive records of church growth in the history of the United States. These figures indicate that the Church of God in Christ is the second largest black organization in America, exceeded only by the National Baptist Convention.

Although the Church of God in Christ did not play a major role in the black civil rights movements of the 1950s and 1960s, many Church of God in Christ ministers and members stood at the side of Martin Luther King in his non-violent crusade for equal rights. In fact it was in Memphis' Mason Temple that King preached his famous "I have been to the Mountain" message. This, his last sermon, was delivered the night before his assassination. Furthermore, the site of his death was the Lorraine Motel, owned by a leading Memphis lay member of the Church of God in Christ.

In recent years, the charismatic movement has been

conspicuous for its apparent lack of success with blacks in the mainline churches. But the Pentecostal movement has positively flourished in the predominantly black Church of God in Christ. In the last decades of the twentieth century, Patterson's fast-growing church continued to serve as a haven for the masses.

A footnote to this story is that the Church of Christ (Holiness), founded by C.P. Jones in 1907 in rejection of the Pentecostal experience, continues until this day. A comparison of the records of the two churches since then is instructive about the power of Pentecost for church growth. In 1964, Jones' church reported only 7,621 members in 146 churches while the Church of God in Christ had grown to over 400,000 members in more than 4,000 congregations. The only difference between the two was the releasing of the power of the Holy Spirit in the Church of God in Christ with signs and wonders following.[17]

The story of Mason and his Church of God in Christ is truly one of the great success stories of church growth in modern America.

For further information on the Church of God in Christ, write:
Bishop Ithiel Clemmons
190-08 104th Ave.
Hollis, NY 11412

CHAPTER SEVEN

The Episcopal Renewal

At nine o'clock in the morning, on a November day in 1959, Dennis Bennett, rector of St. Mark's Episcopal Church in Van Nuys, California, knelt in the home of some friends and began to pray in tongues. Unknown to Bennett, this experience of being baptized in the Holy Spirit was destined to change his life forever. Furthermore, the major churches of Christendom were to be moved strangely in the years to come by this event.[1]

In a way, Bennett was at the opposite pole of the people called Pentecostals who championed the experience they called baptism in the Holy Spirit. For them this was often a cataclysmic baptism which was evidenced by glossolalia or speaking in tongues. Most surveys of American opinion placed Episcopalians at the top of the list of respectable Christians, while the lowly Pentecostals usually occupied the bottom rung on the social ladder.[2]

The aftermath of Bennett's experience was remarkable in that many members of his parish also received the Pentecostal experience and saw their lives and spiritual devotion completely changed. In April 1960, Bennett shared his experience with the members of his wealthy parish. What followed was almost a riot of rejection. "We are Episcopalians, not a bunch of wild-eyed hillbillies," shouted a speaker from a chair used as a soapbox. "Throw out the damned tongues-speakers," yelled another.[3]

To make a long story short, Bennett did resign shortly, but not before the newspapers and *Time* and *Newsweek* magazines gave such national publicity to the event that Bennett became a controversial figure overnight. He also became the leader of a new force in the traditional denominations which was called the neo-Pentecostal movement. *Time* magazine reported that "now glosso-lalia seems to be on its way back in U.S. churches—not only in the uninhibited Pentecostal sects, but even among the Episcopalians, who have been called 'God's frozen people.' "[4]

Although Bennett's case was striking and made head-lines around the world, he was not the first clergyman in his church to speak in tongues and remain in the ministry. With varying degrees of success, at least two of his colleagues had preceded him in experiencing Pentecostal phenomena.

In 1907, after the Azusa Street revival had awakened the world to the gifts of the Spirit, Alexander Boddy, vicar of All Soul's Church in Sunderland, England, had fostered a Pentecostal revival in his church. For several years the annual Sunderland Conventions became centers for church renewal in England, Europe and the United States. This "renewal that failed" was ended mainly because of World War I and a lack of able leader-ship. As Boddy's many followers—some were

Methodists, Baptists, Plymouth Brethren and the Salvation Army—saw that Pentecostalism seemed unlikely to change the British mainline churches, they departed to form new Pentecostal denominations in Britain, notably the Assemblies of God and the Elim Pentecostal Church.

Michael Harper speaks of Boddy as a "prophet few listened to, and most forgot." The first Anglican Pentecostal, Boddy moved from Sunderland in 1922 to become vicar of Pittington, which was located in the same diocese. He remained there until his death in 1929, a man clearly ahead of his time.[5]

Richard Winkler and Dennis Bennett

In 1956, an American Episcopal priest, Richard Winkler, rector of the Trinity Episcopal Church in Wheaton, Illinois, was baptized in the Holy Spirit and spoke in tongues. He was probably the first Episcopal pastor in America to espouse the movement openly. His ministry was so revolutionized after receiving the Pentecostal baptism that healing services were held in his church and many members received the Pentecostal experience.[6]

Because of Bennett's and Winkler's experiences, the Episcopal church issued three reports in the 1960s to deal with the growing movement in the church. The first one appeared in April 1960 in response to Bennett's experience. This document adopted the dispensational view that tongues belonged to the infancy of the church and were discarded like scaffolding after the church came to maturity. Winkler's case also elicited a report in December 1960 which warned of diabolic deception and sectarianism. While recognizing that glossolalia could be genuine, the report stated that "reason is supremely

the voice of the Holy Ghost...." Despite this pronounce-
ment, Winkler was allowed to remain in his church and
make it an early center for charismatic activity in the
Midwest.[7]

The reaction to Bennett's experience was so explosive
that his baptism in the Spirit became a true baptism of
fire. Because of his suffering and later vindication, he
is widely regarded as the father of the charismatic movement in the mainline churches.

The movement spread rapidly into the Episcopal
churches of Southern California after Bennett's case
became well known. By 1963 *Christianity Today* spoke
of a new penetration in which 2,000 Episcopalians in
Southern California were said to be speaking in
tongues.[8]

These new Pentecostals were somewhat different from
the older classical Pentecostals, explained Jean Stone,
an early leader in the movement. They were less emo-
tional and used their gifts more privately as a prayer
language. They also violated many stereotypes about
Pentecostalism that had been held widely for decades.
They were made up primarily of well-educated clergy
and lay professionals. Also their services were quite
orderly and paid much attention to Paul's directions
about the decent and orderly use of the gifts.[9]

The ecclesiastical response to Bennett's experience
was swift and negative. His ecclesiastical superior,
Bishop Francis Bloy, not only forbade tongues-speaking
in St. Mark's, but banned their use in all the parishes
of his diocese. Elsewhere in California, Bishop James
A. Pike issued a 2,500-word letter to all 125 parishes
of his diocese forbidding glossolalia in the churches.
Calling the movement "heresy in embryo," he stated

that "this particular phenomenon has reached a point where it is dangerous to the peace and unity of the church...." These statements notwithstanding, there was no stopping the move of the Spirit in the Episcopal churches of California and other states. [10]

Despite his prohibition of tongues in the services of his diocese, Pike was occasionally greeted with congregations and priests who would burst out singing in tongues during his regular rounds of the churches. Ironically, this same Bishop Pike later ended his ecclesiastical career in disgrace after a vain search to communicate with the dead through the medium of spiritualism.

Other more friendly voices were heard in the church. After hearing about the plight of Bennett, William Fisher Lewis, bishop of Olympia, Washington, invited him to assume the pastorate of St. Luke's Episcopal Church, a run-down urban parish near Seattle. Since consideration had already been given to closing St. Luke's, Lewis invited Bennett to come and "bring the fire" with him. With this permission to teach and express his Pentecostal modes of worship and praise, Bennett and his church were soon in the midst of a tremendous spiritual renewal.

St. Luke's in Seattle

St. Luke's became a center of charismatic renewal, not only for the Episcopal Church, but also for many churches and pastors from various denominations in the Northwestern United States. In a short time, his entire vestry and most of the membership of the church had been baptized in the Holy Spirit. Although the Sunday morning services were quite traditional, the Tuesday night prayer meetings were packed with people and

Pentecostal power. For many years, hundreds of persons attended services weekly at St. Luke's, with an average of twenty persons being baptized in the Holy Spirit each week. And these were not Episcopalians only; hundreds were Baptists, Methodists, Catholics and Presbyterians.

In a short time, St. Luke's was the largest Episcopal congregation in the entire Northwestern region of the United States. Offerings were multiplied as the church changed from an urban liability to a dynamic spiritual center.[11]

Bennett's experiences were widely publicized in the press, thus drawing attention to the growing Pentecostal movement in the Episcopal Church. His example encouraged hundreds of other clergymen to come out of the closet and testify to their experiences in the Holy Spirit.

These Spirit-baptized clergymen were Pentecostals, to be sure, but they wanted to remain in their church and lead their co-religionists in a spiritual renewal. They differed from their brothers in the traditional Pentecostal denominations such as the Assemblies of God, yet they shared in the same dynamic experiences in the Holy Spirit. Though many Episcopal pastors such as Winkler, and ministers in other churches such as Harald Bredesen and James Brown, had received their Pentecostal experiences before he had, Bennett was recognized as the pioneer of the neo-Pentecostal movement because of the publicity surrounding his case.

Another important early center for the Episcopal renewal soon developed in the Church of the Redeemer in Houston, Texas. Here Graham Pulkingham led his congregation in an experiment in charismatic parish renewal, an example which served as a model for many other churches. The rapid growth of the parish with its unique community life and social ministries attracted national attention. Many Episcopal leaders, as well as pastors from other denominations traveled to Houston to see how Pentecostal worship could be integrated into the full liturgical and sacramental life of the church.[12]

To aid the struggling new movement in the church, a new publication appeared in 1961 with the title *Trinity*, edited by Jean Stone. This, the first neo-Pentecostal paper in the United States, featured many Episcopal leaders and writers. It also acted as the voice of the Blessed Trinity Society, a new organization which was founded to foster the ministry of healing in the church and functioned from 1961 to 1966. This was the first organized charismatic society in an American mainline denomination.[13]

Worldwide Anglican Renewal

Further help came from a 1962 study of the Episcopal bishops which was published in the *Journal of the General Convention*. Referring to new movements in the church, the bishops affirmed that "God's Spirit is ever moving in new ways" and the "new movements have in history enriched the body of Christ." Observing that the church "should not be a sect, but should be spacious," the bishops nevertheless counseled against "self-righteousness, divisiveness, one-sidedness and ex-aggeration." The renewal should, therefore, relate itself to the "full, rich, balanced life of the historic church," said the bishops.[14]

This statement became the official policy of the church toward the neo-Pentecostal movement and opened the door to wide acceptance and participation of charismatics in the church. After 1962, the movement did indeed spread rapidly in the church, not only in America, but around the world.

In England, a group of evangelicals led by Canon Michael Harper established the Fountain Trust, an ecumenical body of charismatics in all the churches, but mainly led by Anglicans. In other nations, bishops and archbishops became involved, the most important one being Archbishop William Burnett of Capetown, South Africa. Other important leaders were Bishop Festo Kivengere of Uganda, Bishops Chitemo and Madina of Tanzania, Archbishop Manassas Kuria of Kenya, Bishop Derek Rawcliffe of the New Hebrides Islands, and Ban it Chiu, bishop of Singapore. The influence of the movement was widespread and influential.[15]

In Atlanta, Georgia, David Collins, canon of the largest Episcopal parish in the United States, became a national leader in the movement. Other leaders included Bishop William Frey of Colorado, Robert Hawn, Everett (Terry) Fullam and Charles M. Irish. To coordinate this growing force in the American church, in 1973 these men formed the Episcopal Charismatic Fellowship. This body soon published a journal entitled *Acts 29* which became a clearinghouse for information about the movement.[16]

By the mid-1970s, the Episcopal and Anglican movements, along with most other mainline churches, had abandoned the name neo-Pentecostal movement for the more neutral term charismatic renewal. Also, to escape the cultural baggage of classical Pentecostalism, Episcopal leaders began to develop an organic theology of the baptism in the Holy Spirit which emphasized the work of the Holy Spirit throughout the Christian life, as well as in the initial personal experience of being baptized in the Holy Spirit. Charismatic Episcopalians also drew on the ancient creeds of the church for their experiences in the Holy Spirit.

A New Canterbury Tale

With a wide measure of acceptance within the Anglican communion, Anglican charismatics planned an international conference at Canterbury in 1978 to precede the meeting of the Lambeth Conference. Lambeth is the most important gathering of Anglicanism, where all the bishops meet only once every decade. During the week before Lambeth, about 500 charismatic leaders gathered at the University of Kent at Canterbury. A week of prayer and workshops preceded the closing services in the historic cathedral. In the first service, Archbishop of Canterbury Donald Coggan addressed the delegates warmly.

The closing liturgy was so wondrous that it is still referred to as "a new Canterbury tale." Led by Archbishop Burnett, the three-hour service included tongues, prophecies, prayer for the sick, and great rejoicing. This all took place within the context of a traditional Anglican communion service.

At the close of this historic gathering, the 2,000 worshippers joined in a time of rejoicing as the Spirit was poured out in Pentecostal fullness. Canterbury truly became a new upper room. The ancient walls of the cathedral echoed to the shouts of praise that swelled from the hearts of the congregation. Thirty-two bishops and archbishops dancing around the high altar in high praise of the Lord was an unforgettable sight.[17]

After 1978, the movement continued to spread among Anglican churches and mission fields around the world.

In some cases, entire national churches were swept by the movement. The church in the New Hebrides was one such case. At Canterbury, Bishop Rawcliffe told of all his churches and priests being deeply affected by a revival of the charismatic gifts. In England, David Watson told of overflow crowds at his services in York, which included great crowds filling the cathedral for charismatic services.

Some African bishops, such as Festo Kivengere, could not recall a time when their national Anglican churches were anything but charismatic. This was especially true of those churches touched by the great East African revivals of the 1930s.

In America, Everett Fullam, vicar of St. Paul's Church in Darien, Connecticut, experienced overflow crowds as the Spirit moved in his regular services. The "miracle at Darien" was repeated at numerous other Episcopal churches in America.[18]

Three Northern Virginia parishes experienced extraordinary growth in the early 1980s when they decided to go the charismatic route. The Falls Church and Truro parishes were two of Virginia's oldest colonial Episcopal parishes. Yet they took on new life as the Holy Spirit was poured out among their members. In the same area, the Church of the Apostles experienced extraordinary growth. Under the leadership of Rector Renny Scott, this church grew from fifty in attendance to over 2,000 in only seven years. Theirs has been described as an "exuberant charismatic parish."[19]

By 1984 a survey showed that out of 7,200 Episcopal parishes in the United States, over 400 were involved in the charismatic renewal. Some of these were the fastest-growing churches in the denomination.

The Episcopal charismatic movement in the United States is directed by Episcopal Renewal Ministries, under the leadership of Everett L. Fullam and Charles M. Irish.

For more information and literature contact:
Episcopal Renewal Ministries
Charles M. Irish, National Coordinator
10520 Main Street
Fairfax, VA 22030
(703) 273-8660

CHAPTER EIGHT

The Foursquare Church

In July 1922 the world-famous evangelist, Aimee Semple McPherson, stood in the Oakland Civic Auditorium in California, and shared a vision which in time became the International Church of the Foursquare Gospel. Preaching from Ezekiel 1:4-28, which describes a creature with four faces, she saw in that passage four major doctrines. They were symbolized in the man, the lion, the ox and the eagle, and they became the core of her ministry.

The evangelist went on to tell of the vision she had which clarified the meaning of the faces. She said they all represented Jesus: the face of the man was Jesus as Savior; the lion was Jesus as baptizer in the Holy Spirit; the ox was Jesus as healer; and the eagle was Jesus as the coming king. She described this revelation as ''a perfect gospel, a complete gospel for body, for soul, for spirit and for eternity.'' Thus was born the theology and the name for a major Pentecostal denomination which today ministers in fifty-five nations of the world under the banner of the International Church of the

Foursquare Gospel.[1]

It has been said that an institution is the lengthened shadow of a man. In this case, it is the lengthened shadow of a woman.

Sister Aimee

Aimee Semple McPherson was born in Ingersoll, Ontario, Canada, in 1890. She holds a prominent rank among all religious leaders in the twentieth century regardless of their sex and may well be the most important ordained woman minister in the history of Christianity. A flamboyant, talented and attractive woman, she commanded the attention of the world for over two decades. Her early years were chronicled in her 1927 autobiography, *In the Service of the King*.

Aimee's father was a Methodist, but her early religious training came from her mother, Minnie Kennedy, who served as a leader in the Salvation Army. Despite being raised in the Holiness tradition, Aimee was converted as a teenager in 1907 in a revival conducted by a young Pentecostal evangelist named Robert Semple. Soon after that, Aimee was baptized in the Holy Spirit and spoke in tongues. She left the Salvation Army to become a Pentecostal, and she also fell in love with the evangelist and married him.[2]

The young couple accepted a call to go to the Orient as missionaries. In 1910 they arrived in China and were there only a few short months when Semple died. Aimee was then eight months pregnant with her first child. Returning to the United States, she worked in the Salvation Army with her mother in New York City. In 1912, she married Harold Stewart McPherson of Providence, Rhode Island. They had a son, Rolf Kennedy McPherson, who was destined to become president of the church in 1944.

Aimee's marriage to McPherson was an unhappy one—she felt called to hit the sawdust trail while he wished to continue as a businessman. They were later divorced. In 1915, "Sister Aimee," as she was affectionately known, answered the call to evangelize after holding a successful revival crusade in Mount Forest, Ontario. By 1918, after a whirlwind tour of revivals up and down the East Coast, she settled down in Los Angeles where she lived for the rest of her life.[3]

It took several years, however, before the restless evangelist was able to settle on a denominational home in which to minister. Before founding the Foursquare movement, she joined at least three churches in addition to the Salvation Army in which she was born. In December 1920 she united with the Hancock Methodist Episcopal Church in Philadelphia. In March 1922 Pastor William Keeney Towner ordained her as a Baptist minister in the First Baptist Church in San Jose, California. And for several years she was listed as a minister of the Assemblies of God. All of these affiliations lapsed when she founded her own denomination in 1927.[4]

Angelus Temple

During the latter part of the 1920s, Aimee became an institution as well as a pastor and evangelist. With a national magazine called *The Bridal Call* (now known as *Foursquare World Advance*) and with the financial support that came from her continuing salvation-healing crusades, she began construction of the Angelus Temple near Echo Park in Los Angeles in 1921. This sanctuary—the largest church in America at the time with 5,300 seats—became the center of her burgeoning ministry. Its value was $1.5 million (in 1921 dollars!).[5]

During the first year in the temple, more than 10,000 persons answered altar calls to be born again. For the next twenty years the temple was usually filled to capacity with persons anxious to see and hear the legendary woman evangelist. Thousands of people were often turned away for lack of seats. In those years, Aimee ministered to more than 20,000 persons per Sunday. It was America's first "superchurch."

Aimee's ministry continued to skyrocket after the dedication of the temple in 1923. She was the first woman to preach a sermon over the radio (1922) and the first pastor to build a radio station owned by a local church. The station went on the air in 1924 with the call letters KFSG (Kall Foursquare Gospel). This was the first Christian radio station in America. In 1925, she also opened a Bible school housed in a five-story building constructed next to the church. The school was called L.I.F.E Bible College (Lighthouse International Foursquare Evangelism), an institution founded with a mandate to train the hundreds of new young leaders who flocked to her church.[6]

The ministries of Aimee Semple McPherson and Angelus Temple were staggering. In the beginning, she personally conducted twenty-one services per week for the faithful. Her dramatic services captured the imagination and curiosity of the public. She often wrote the dramas, pageants and oratorios that were presented by the huge staff of the temple. In one typical service, Sister Aimee drove onto the huge stage on a motorcycle dressed as a policeman, blew a whistle and shouted, "Stop, you are going to hell!" In another service, the stage was set as a cotton plantation in the Old South with overtones of "Gone With the Wind" modified to proclaim the Foursquare gospel. These extravaganzas made her a celebrity from coast to coast, with her activities gaining press attention equal to that of any Hollywood star.[7]

All was not drama and glamour at the temple, however. In 1926 the Angelus Temple Commissary was opened to feed the hungry and clothe the naked. When the Depression hit the nation after 1929, the temple fed and clothed over 1.5 million needy people in the Los Angeles area. Because of her love for the poor, Sister Aimee won the everlasting love and devotion of the down and outers of depressed America. Among those attracted to the evangelist in those hard times were movie star Anthony Quinn and Richard Halverson, who later served as chaplain of the U.S. Senate. The most famous person ever to "walk the aisles" in Angelus Temple was a young Quaker boy by the name of Richard Milhous Nixon.[8]

In May 1926 Aimee disappeared from a beach near Los Angeles, and her whereabouts were unknown for several weeks. When she reappeared in June in New Mexico, she claimed to have been kidnapped. Many rumors circulated about "the vanishing evangelist," but in a subsequent court case, she was acquitted of any fraud or wrongdoing. In later years she was also involved in sensational lawsuits with her mother, Minnie, who also served as her business manager. The dauntless Aimee, however, survived these crises as well as others and each time went on to ever greater victories.[9]

Church of the Foursquare Gospel

With her growing and dynamic ministry attracting thousands of faithful followers throughout the United

States, Aimee organized her own denomination in 1927. True to her 1922 vision, it was called the International Church of the Foursquare Gospel with headquarters at Angelus Temple. The new church was identical to the Assemblies of God in doctrine, while differing in organizational structure and polity. Under Sister Aimee's tight control, the denomination developed a strongly centralized structure with all church properties owned by the parent corporation.[10]

The Foursquare doctrinal statement placed it in the mainstream of the American Pentecostal movement. Trinitarian and evangelical, the church adopted the "initial evidence" theory of glossolalia as constituting the first sign of receiving the baptism in the Holy Spirit. The idea of four major doctrinal statements had been used earlier by A.B. Simpson of the Christian and Missionary Alliance, who had spoken of Jesus as "savior, sanctifier, healer and coming king." The only difference in the Foursquare statement was the substitution of "baptizer in the Holy Spirit" for "sanctifier." Aimee also compiled a Declaration of Faith consisting of twenty-two articles which elaborated on the four fundamental teachings of the church.[11]

The early days of the new organization saw explosive growth as many independent Pentecostal congregations applied to join the movement. By 1928 there were over fifty Foursquare churches in Southern California with scores of others throughout the United States applying to join. Soon missionaries were carrying the Foursquare banner to Canada, Britain and many other nations. The main reason for this early growth was the magnetic and dynamic personality of the foundress.[12]

Aimee often traveled to the missionary field. In 1943

she was on such a trip in Mexico when she contacted a tropical fever. A year later, on September 22, 1944, she died after preaching a sermon in Oakland, California. Her death certificate indicated she had died from "shock and respiratory failure" after she took sleeping capsules prescribed by a doctor.

The Church After Aimee

After her death, leadership passed to her son, Rolf, who has served as president ever since. To carry on the administration of the organization, McPherson relied on a general field supervisor and district supervisors for the United States; they carried out the day-to-day affairs of the denomination. In addition, a director of world missions was given supervision of the church's foreign missionaries. The best known of the general supervisors was Howard P. Courtney who served the church from 1944 to 1974. Others who have served since Courtney are M.E. Nichols, Roy Hicks Sr. and Eugene Kurtz, who succeeded Hicks in 1986. McPherson's vice president is Harold Helms, who also serves as pastor of Angelus Temple.[13]

Since 1927, the growth of the church has been steady though not as spectacular as in the early days. By 1944, the number of congregations in the United States had reached 500. After a period of slow growth in the 1950s and 1960s, the church experienced a revival and renewal in the 1970s and 1980s during the time of the charismatic renewal in the mainline churches. By 1985, the number of churches in the United States had surpassed 1,200. Of all the classical Pentecostal denominations, the Foursquare church has been the most affected by the charismatic renewal. To many outsiders, the worship services of the church are such that charismatics from mainline denominations feel immediately at home.[14]

A great impetus in this development has been the ministry of Jack Hayford, whose Church on the Way in Van Nuys, California, has grown to be the largest Foursquare congregation in the United States. With over 6,000 members, his church is a modern-day counterpart to Angelus Temple. Hayford's influence reaches far beyond the bounds of his denomination, however, since he is a popular speaker for many charismatic conferences.

In recent years, the church has emphasized education more than in the past. In addition to L.I.F.E Bible College, the Foursquare Church operates the Mount Vernon Bible College in Ohio. Also there is a greater interest in theology as Foursquare students enroll in major universities and seminaries around the nation. A major theology of the church was published in 1983 by L.I.F.E Bible College. Written by Guy Duffield and Nathaniel Van Cleave, it is entitled *Foundations of Pentecostal Theology*.[15]

The greatest American growth for the church in recent years has taken place in the Northwestern states where Roy Hicks Jr. has led in planting many churches in Oregon and Washington. Other significant growth has taken place in California and the East. By 1986, some of the largest Foursquare churches in America included: Jack Hayford's Church on the Way in Van Nuys, California; Ron Mehl's Foursquare congregation in Beaverton, Oregon; and the Faith Center church in Eugene, Oregon, pastored by Roy Hicks Jr. At least two Foursquare congregations own television stations. These are operated by the Foursquare churches in Decatur, Illinois, and Roanoke, Virginia.[16]

For most of its history the American church was larger than the churches on the mission fields. In 1952, for instance, only one third of the church's members lived outside the United States. By 1960 the numbers were approximately equal. By 1985, however, more than two thirds of the church membership lived overseas. The figures for that year were 181,594 members in the United States and 863,642 in other countries. The grand total of members, affiliates and adherents worldwide in 1985 stood at 1,045,236 persons.[17]

At the annual convention in 1986, McPherson reported that during the previous year 354,110 persons had made "decisions for Christ" in Foursquare churches around the world. Of these, 84,004 had been baptized in water, while 92,848 had received the baptism in the Holy Ghost. The total number of churches and meeting places where these spiritual experiences took place stood at 12,628. By 1986 a new Foursquare church was opened somewhere in the world every six hours.[18]

Serving these churches is a ministerium of 4,856 pastors, evangelists and missionaries around the world. Of these, 737 are ordained women, many of whom serve as pastors. In fact, the 1986 minutes indicate that no less than 41 percent of all the ordained Foursquare ministers in the United States are women, one of the highest proportions of women ministers of any church in the world. This large percentage may reflect the fact that a woman, with roots in the Salvation Army, founded the church.[19]

The year of 1988 will stand out as a crossroads for Foursquaredom—Rolf McPherson is scheduled to retire at the annual convention. For the first time in history a McPherson will not be at the helm of the church. Since McPherson was president for life, his retirement will probably call for basic structural changes in the government of the church. With his retirement, an era will come to an end in the history of American Pentecostalism.[20]

For further information on the International Church of the Foursquare Gospel, contact:
Eugene Kurtz
International Church of the Foursquare Gospel
1100 Glendale Boulevard
Los Angeles, CA 90026-3282
Phone: (213) 484-1100

CHAPTER NINE

The Lutheran Renewal

In 1947 a young Lutheran layman in New York City noticed a growing local Pentecostal congregation where hundreds of people from all denominational backgrounds gathered to receive healing and to experience what they called the baptism in the Holy Spirit. Although he was an official of the World Council of Christian Education headquartered in Manhattan, the young man felt irresistibly drawn to investigate the unusual services that attracted so many people in the big city.

Soon the young Lutheran joined the crowds at the altar seeking the baptism. In a short time he received the Pentecostal experience and arose speaking in a new language he had not learned. The young man was named Harald Bredesen and the church was an Assemblies of God congregation pastored by P.G. Emmett.[1]

This man Bredesen was destined to be a John the Baptist for the charismatic renewal movement in the mainline denominational churches. He was one of the earliest ministers outside the classical Pentecostal movement to experience glossolalia and continue in the ministry of a traditional non-Pentecostal church.

Bredesen had been born and raised a thoroughgoing Lutheran with plans of entering a Lutheran pastorate after his work ended with the staff of the World Council of Christian Education in New York. The son of a Lutheran pastor in Minnesota, he had attended Luther Theological Seminary in St. Paul and had served a pastoral internship in Aberdeen, South Dakota, before coming to his position in New York.

In later years, Bredesen was to influence many important Christian leaders to experience the baptism in the Holy Spirit, including Pat Robertson, John Sherrill and Pat Boone. He was ordained a minister in the Dutch Reformed Church and accepted a call to pastor a Dutch Reformed congregation in Mt. Vernon, New York. In the 1960s, he also led many of his parishioners into the Pentecostal experience. In 1963, he was instrumental in leading a sensational meeting at Yale University where many students also spoke in tongues. They were jokingly called ''glossoyalies'' by the press.[2]

By the 1980s Bredesen was well known as a friend to President Sadat of Egypt as well as an advisor to his old friend and protege Pat Robertson in his bid for the Republican nomination for the presidency of the United States. In the long run, however, Bredesen may be best known as one of the earliest neo-Pentecostals who served as a harbinger of things to come in the mainline denominations.[3]

Larry Christenson

Larry Christenson was one of the first Lutherans to experience the baptism in the Holy Spirit in the 1960s. Only a year out of seminary and in his first pastorate,

Trinity Lutheran Church (ALC) in San Pedro, California, Christenson had been fascinated by the possibility of divine healing through an earlier reading of Agnes Sanford's book *The Healing Light*.

Attending a revival service in a Foursquare Pentecostal Church in San Pedro, he heard about the baptism in the Holy Spirit evidenced by speaking in tongues. The evangelists, Wayne and Mary Westburg, prayed for him, but nothing happened. That night, however, the young Lutheran pastor awakened out of sleep, "sat bolt-upright in bed and found an unknown tongue" hovering on his lips. He spoke a sentence in tongues and then fell back to sleep. This was on Friday morning, August 4, 1961. The next night he returned to the Foursquare church where he reported that a "great sense of praise and joy began to well up within me, and it spilled over my lips in a new tongue." It was a wonderful experience, he said, "though not a particularly overwhelming one."

Christenson was immediately concerned with the question of whether this experience was Lutheran or not and about his future as a Lutheran pastor. In a later conversation with David du Plessis, he was advised to stay in the Lutheran church and spread the renewal among his peers.[4]

The Character of Lutherans

Historically, Lutherans have been primarily concerned with matters coming out of the Protestant Reformation. These include such basic principles as justification by faith and the primacy of the Scriptures.

In many ways Martin Luther was as conservative as he was a revolutionary. In the reformation, he went so far and no further. His opposition to the Peasants' War and the Anabaptist movement indicated his conservatism. He held in special contempt the enthusiasts he called the "schwarmerei." He was also quite critical of the claims to miracles which he regarded as Roman Catholic superstition. Although it has been said that Luther spoke in tongues, there is no credible contemporary evidence to support this claim.

Indeed, Luther heartily subscribed to the cessation theory which held that the signs, wonders and miracles of the New Testament ceased after the age of the apostles. Thus, if one spoke in tongues in modern times, he would probably not be considered to be a typical Lutheran.[5]

Others Receive the Baptism

Despite Lutheran tradition, the early 1960s saw a veritable flood of Lutherans who received the Pentecostal experience. All the branches of American Lutheranism were affected, including the American Lutheran Church (ALC), the Lutheran Church in America (LCA) and the Lutheran Church, Missouri Synod (LCMS).

An interesting testimony came from Erwin Prange, a pastor who was baptized in the Holy Spirit in the sanctuary of his church on a morning in 1963 just before leading a confirmation class. As he prayed, a voice seemed to say, "The gift is already yours; just reach out and take it." Then, stretching his hands toward the altar, "I opened my mouth, and strange babbling sounds rushed forth. Had I done it? Or was it the Spirit? Before I had time to wonder, all sorts of strange things began to happen. God came out of the shadows. 'He is real!' I thought. 'He is here!' He loves me!...every cell and atom of my body tingled with the vibrant life of God."

When he went to teach his confirmation class, he talked for ten minutes in a language neither he nor his hearers could understand.[6]

Leading pastors who received the baptism in this period included Herbert Mjorud, who was serving as a full-time evangelist of the ALC in 1962 after visiting Dennis Bennett's Episcopal Church in Seattle. Afterward he was amazed to see a healing ministry break out in his evangelistic crusades. In a revival in Anacortes, Washington, in March 1962, over seventy Lutherans were baptized in the Holy Spirit. As a result of this meeting, Mjorud was accused of heresy by several pastors.

After his answer to the president of the denomination, all charges were dropped. But his call as an ALC evangelist was not renewed, and he became an independent evangelist. His later years were distinguished by mass healing crusades in many nations of the world.[7]

Mjorud was not alone in being investigated by church authorities. In 1963 the ALC appointed a commission of three to investigate the persons involved with glossolalia in the church. This team consisted of a psychologist, a psychiatrist and a New Testament theologian. In San Pedro, the team examined Christenson and thirty-two members of his congregation. A control group of twenty tongues-speakers was compared with another group of non-tongues-speakers. Although the team expected the Pentecostals to be "unstable people emotionally" and that the movement would be "short lived," they were wrong on both counts. The results were published in the book entitled *The Psychology of Speaking in Tongues* by John Kildahl (the clinical psychologist in the study).[8]

Throughout the 1960s and '70s, hundreds of Lutheran pastors and thousands of laypersons entered into the Pentecostal experience. Among these were Donald Pfotenhauer, Erwin Prange, Robert Heil, Rodney Lensch, Delbert Rossin, Herb Mirly and Theodore Jungkuntz of the Lutheran Church, Missouri Synod. In the American Lutheran Church, Morris Vaagenes, James Hanson and George Voeks joined Christenson and Mjorud as leaders in the movement.

The Lutheran Church in America was not as deeply affected as the other branches. Yet by 1970, Paul Swedeberg and Glen Pearson were leading charismatic renewal movements in their local churches.[9]

Many of these pastors suffered varying degrees of acceptance or rejection from their ecclesiastical superiors. The most wrenching case of rejection was that experienced by Don Pfotenhauer, pastor of the Way of the Cross Lutheran Church in Blaine, Minnesota. This congregation was part of the Missouri Synod, one of the most conservative Lutheran bodies in America.

After receiving the baptism in the Holy Spirit in 1964, church authorities attempted to remove him from his pulpit. Though Pfotenhauer tried to stay with his church, a great majority of whom supported him, he was finally excommunicated in 1970. His supporters then organized an independent group with the same name Way of the Cross. His story made headlines for years in the Minneapolis newspapers.[10]

By the early 1970s, because of this case and other similar ones, Lutheran charismatics began to band together to promote the movement in their churches. By 1972, the idea of a national all-Lutheran charismatic conference gained currency among several leaders.

Sparked by Norris Wogen, the first International Lutheran Conference on the Holy Spirit was convened in the Civic Auditorium in Minneapolis. To the delight of the organizers, the auditorium which seated 9,000 persons was filled to capacity as over 10,000 persons registered for the sessions. In the years since 1972, this conference has grown to be the largest annual gathering of Lutherans in the United States.[11]

A Lutheran Charismatic Theology

In time, Lutheran charismatic pastors felt the need to produce a charismatic theology which would situate the Pentecostal experience and phenomena within the Lutheran theological system. In 1976 a book was published by Larry Christenson entitled *The Charismatic Renewal Among Lutherans*. In this volume, Christenson traced the history of the movement and offered what he called an organic view of the baptism in the Holy Spirit (as contrasted to the classical Pentecostal second blessing, initial evidence view).

This book was followed in 1987 with the most ambitious and important theological work yet done within the Lutheran renewal. Edited by Larry Christenson in consultation with forty of his colleagues, it is titled *Welcome, Holy Spirit*. In this work, the International Lutheran Charismatic Theological Consultation leans in the direction of the classical Pentecostal position by recognizing a New Testament distinction between a charismatic sending of the Holy Spirit and the salvific coming of the Spirit at initiation.

In addition to these works, Theodore Jungkuntz has produced some basic works relating the renewal to the theology and sacramental life of the church. These include a 1983 booklet entitled *A Lutheran Charismatic*

Catechism, and in 1983 a theological treatise entitled *Confirmation and the Charismata.*[12]

While the charismatics were developing their theology, the Lutheran denominations were also studying the movement and issuing reports designed to guide pastors in relating to the movement.

The Lutheran Church, Missouri Synod, ordered a report on the movement in April 1968 when it learned that forty-four of its pastors were involved in the renewal. By the time the report was completed in 1972, the number had risen to over 200 pastors. This was to be the most negative Lutheran report of the many that followed around the world. After questioning the possibility of valid manifestations of supernatural gifts and miracles in the modern age, the report declared that "power and renewal are to be sought in the Word and sacraments, not in special signs and miracles."[13]

The *1972 Guidelines* of the American Lutheran Church was much more positive in tone. While cautioning charismatics concerning the proper place of the gifts in the life of believers, the report called for an allowance for diversity which would give liberty for the renewal to develop further within the church.[14]

In 1974, the Lutheran Church in America issued the most positive report of all. Entitled *The Charismatic Movement: A Pastoral Perspective*, this report stated that "there is no cause for Lutheran pastors or people to suggest either explicitly or implicitly that one cannot be charismatic and remain a Lutheran in good standing."[15]

By the 1980s some resistance remained in some Lutheran quarters, but in general charismatic renewal was so accepted that it had become part of the Lutheran landscape.

Lutheran Charismatic Organizations

After the 1972 Minneapolis conference, Lutheran charismatic leaders set up permanent organizations to promote the work of the renewal. In 1973 Lutheran Charismatic Renewal Services was formed under the leadership of Larry Christenson and Dick Denny, an ALC layman. By the end of the 1970s the North Heights Lutheran Church in St. Paul, Minnesota, emerged as an important center for Lutheran renewal. Under the leadership of Pastor Morris Vaagenes and W. Dennis Pederson, the International Lutheran Center for Church Renewal was formed in 1980.[16]

By 1983, these two service organizations were merged and offices were located in the North Heights church in St. Paul. The name of the merged group was changed to the International Lutheran Renewal Center with Larry Christenson as the full-time director. Also working on the staff with Christenson are Dick Denny, Betty Denny, Dennis Pederson and Del Rossin.[17]

Status of Lutheran Renewal

The 1979 Gallup Poll conducted for *Christianity Today* estimated that twenty percent of all American Lutherans identify with the charismatic/Pentecostal renewal. This same poll showed that three percent of all American Lutherans speak with tongues. Most estimates are that from ten percent to twenty percent of all Lutherans are involved in the renewal. These figures would indicate that between 1 million and 1.7 million identify with the movement in the United States.[18]

Recent surveys conducted by Fuller Theological Seminary indicate growing participation on the part of

Lutheran pastors in the United States. Figures for all the Lutheran denominations in America in recent years yielded the following results:

	1974	1979	1984	1985
Pastors open	332	466	1000	1295
Pastors charismatic	249	349	751	975
Pastors declared	166	233	501	650[19]

In addition to the American scene, the renewal has moved strongly into Lutheran churches around the world. The Scandinavian Lutheran churches are deeply involved in charismatic renewal as are the Lutheran churches of Germany. Recent reports indicate also that some African Lutheran bishops are moving in the charismatic direction.

In recent years, more and more Lutheran churches have become openly charismatic in their worship services. Several model congregations now exist which could be pointed to as examples of renewal in the Lutheran tradition. One example is Resurrection Lutheran Church (Missouri Synod) in Charlotte, North Carolina. Led into the renewal by Pastor Herb Mirly, this church has developed a unique form of high Lutheran liturgical worship that is enlivened by charismatic prayer and praise.[20]

Other prominent Lutheran congregations in the renewal include Trinity Lutheran Church in San Pedro, California, pastored by Paul Anderson and Faith Lutheran Church in Geneva, Illinois, pastored by Del Rossin.

For more information on the Lutheran renewal write to:
  The International Lutheran Renewal Center
  P.O. Box 13055
  St. Paul, MN 55113
  Phone: (612) 636-7032

CHAPTER TEN

The Mennonite Renewal

O f all the people who have been touched by the renewing power of the Holy Spirit in this century, no one
has been more deeply affected than the Mennonites. The
story of the charismatic renewal among Mennonites is
the story of hundreds of pastors and bishops, and many
thousands of laypersons who have been radically renewed through the baptism in the Holy Spirit.

Like most of the renewals of this century, the Mennonite revival was unplanned, spontaneous and surprising. It all began during a youth "vacation Bible school"
in the Loman Mennonite Church in Minnesota where
seven churches had sent seventy-six teenagers to study
the Bible between Christmas 1954 and New Year's Day,
1955. The leader of this special school was Gerald
Derstine, pastor of the Strawberry Lake Mennonite
Church near Ogema, Minnesota. A "Mennonite of the
Mennonites," Derstine's family had roots in his
denomination that could be traced to the eighteenth century in Pennsylvania.[1]

Gerald Derstine and Strawberry Lake

What happened during those five days and in the months that followed would radically change Derstine's world as well as the Mennonite churches of the world. On the first day of the camp, thirteen unconverted youths in the group were born again after a time of fasting and prayer by the seven pastors in charge. Then, to the puzzlement of the pastors, the phenomenal began to take place.

At first, several children reported hearing angels singing. Afterward, a spirit of intercession for unsaved parents and friends led to fervent prayer for their salvation. Then, quite unexpectedly, some of the children fell prostrate on the floor trembling in a state of ecstasy. The pastors, fearful of demonic activity, began to "plead the blood of Jesus" for protection, but things continued to happen. Others fell to the floor and spoke in tongues.[2]

In short order, these young Mennonites prophesied about impending world events and about a coming world-wide spiritual awakening. One prophesied that Billy Graham would one day preach the gospel behind the Iron Curtain. (This was in 1954!) Some saw visions of Jesus. At times "tongues, prophecy and interpretation flowed like a rushing river," according to Derstine. At other times, singing in tongues filled the plain little Mennonite church with "heavenly melodies." Words of knowledge gave astounding evidence of an unusual "visitation" from God.

Upon returning to his pastorate in Strawberry Lake, Derstine was surprised to see the same charismatic phenomena repeated in homes and in the sanctuary of his church. A prophecy stated that this revival would eventually "affect the entire world." Far from opposing these miraculous manifestations, Derstine accepted them as a fulfillment of Joel's prophecy about the Holy Spirit being poured out "on all flesh" in the last days. He also was baptized in the Holy Spirit, spoke in tongues and experienced many of the same spiritual manifestations himself.

Word spread rapidly in the Mennonite community concerning the strange happenings in Strawberry Lake. Soon bishops and elders of the area began an investigation of Derstine and the events in Loman and Strawberry Lake. By April 1955, the bishops conducted a hearing which resulted in Derstine's being "silenced" from the Mennonite ministry. If only he would admit that some demonic activity had taken place and that some of the manifestations had been "an act of Satan," and if he would promise not to talk about it in the future, Derstine could continue as a Mennonite pastor. This he refused to do.[3]

Later in the year, Derstine met Henry Brunk, a fiery Spirit-filled Mennonite evangelist from Florida who headed the Gospel Crusade Evangelistic Association. By 1959, Derstine had moved to Florida to work with Brunk in developing the Christian Retreat in Bradenton.[4]

The question of the presence of spiritual gifts in Mennonite churches was not settled by the Derstine affair, however. A glance at the long history of Anabaptists and Mennonites was replete with instances of charismatic phenomena similar to those that broke out in Minnesota.

The Mennonite Tradition

The Mennonites arose from among the Anabaptists of the sixteenth century. These rebaptizers, as they were called by their enemies, constituted the most radical of the reformation movements. They taught believer's baptism, as well as separation of church and state. Other Anabaptist views included pacifism and refusal to take oaths in court.

Beginning in Zurich, the Anabaptist movement spread to Germany and Holland. A moderate leader in Holland was Menno Simons, an ex-Roman Catholic priest, who in 1537 assumed a place of leadership among the Anabaptists. His followers eventually became known as Mennonites whose broad family included such groups as the Amish and the Hutterites. Modern Baptists are also heir to the same Anabaptist vision as the Mennonites.[5]

According to Mennonite writer Terry Miller, the early Mennonites were "thoroughly charismatic in the best sense of the word." The story of the church under persecution included many instances of prophecy, dreams, visions and even martyrdom. Anabaptists and Mennonites saw themselves as neither Protestant nor Catholic, and as such were persecuted from all sides. Their vision was not simply a reformation of the church, but a restoration of primitive Christianity. As to the gifts of the Spirit, Menno Simons accepted the presence of all the charisms in church but always insisted that they be tested by Scripture.[6]

Mennonite Charismatics

Four centuries later, the Mennonites, like all other Christians, have been profoundly affected by the modern Pentecostal and charismatic movements. In his book *My Personal Pentecost*, Mennonite charismatic leader Roy Koch has described three phases in Mennonite attitudes toward Pentecostalism: "abomination (pre-1950s), toleration (1960s) and propagation (1970s).'' In the first stage Mennonites sternly opposed the Pentecostal movement. Despite a 1906 statement by Oregon Mennonites calling for a new opening to the baptism in the Holy Spirit, most Mennonites joined other Christians in condemning the Pentecostals. In spite of this attitude, many Mennonites received the experience in these years but remained quiet about it.[7]

Bishop Nelson Litwiller's experience was typical of many in his church. As a missionary to Latin America in the 1920s and 1930s, he was turned off by the style and claims of the Pentecostals he met in Argentina. ''They claimed that they had the power and that we didn't,'' he said. Yet he was impressed by the tremendous growth of the movement in comparison to the relatively slow growth of the other evangelical churches.[8]

Derstine's rejection by the church leaders in Strawberry Lake also demonstrated the attitudes of most Mennonites during this period. Nevertheless, during the 1960s and 1970s several thousand Mennonites received the baptism in the Holy Spirit. They were influenced more by the general charismatic awakening in the mainline churches than by Derstine's experiences. The story of Litwiller is a case in point. His acceptance of the baptism in the Holy Spirit came through Spirit-filled Roman Catholics in South Bend, Indiana. Through the influence of Kevin Ranaghan and others, the venerable missionary bishop was transformed through the Holy Spirit and became a national leader in the movement.[9]

Other important Mennonite leaders were swept into the movement in the same decade, including Roy Koch, Bishop Elam Glick, Herb Minnich, Terry Miller, Allen

Yoder, Dan Yutzy, George Brunk, Fred Augsburger and Harold Gingerich. This period of toleration during the 1960s saw the Mennonite churches accepting the orthodoxy and validity of these charismatic leaders who carefully expressed a rock-ribbed loyalty to their church, despite their Pentecostal experiences.[10]

This phase of toleration soon led into Koch's third stage, that of propagation, or the aggressive promotion of the charismatic movement within the churches with the cautious but clear approval of the ecclesiastical leaders. This period, beginning in the 1970s, saw the inauguration of organized efforts to bring charismatic renewal to the churches.

In 1971, a report was approved by the Lancaster Conference, one of the largest and most conservative regional groups in the nation. This report called for acceptance of "unhindered manifestation of the Spirit's presence through the vibrant expression of praise and the fearless spreading of the good news of the mighty works of God taking place in our time." This report led to a major study of the Holy Spirit and the gifts of the Spirit in the Mennonite Church, the largest of the American Mennonite bodies. This document, which was adopted by the general assembly in July 1977, recognized both strengths and potential weaknesses in the charismatic movement within the church, with the strengths outweighing the weaknesses.[11]

The strengths included "a release of spiritual gifts and power; a strong effective ministry of evangelism; great unity and love among the brotherhood; new forms of community and local church life; miracles of healing; winning the active support of many young people who would otherwise be lost to Christ and the church;

the rediscovery of tongues, the gift of knowledge and other spiritual gifts; a commitment to work within existing churches rather than to separate from them; a great love for Jesus Christ our Lord, and for His church as His body." Potential weaknesses included the possibility of "religious arrogance" and a "careless use of Scripture."[12]

In this new climate of acceptance, the Mennonite charismatics organized service groups to conduct renewal conferences around the United States and Canada. Although an early consultation of charismatic leaders was held in 1972, the major arm of the renewal emerged in 1975.

Mennonite Renewal Services

This organization came as a result of letters sent to Litwiller and Harold Bauman from Kevin Ranaghan inviting the Mennonites to participate in a great ecumenical conference in Kansas City in 1977. Litwiller then invited a group of Mennonite charismatic leaders to meet in Youngstown, Ohio, to consider the invitation. At this meeting the Mennonite Renewal Services was born. The founders of the group included Nelson Litwiller, Dan Yutzy, Harold Bauman, Roy Koch, Herbert Minnich and Fred Augsburger. Since that time, MRS has served as the charismatic arm of the Mennonite Church.[13]

In 1977, Mennonites and Baptists joined together in the Kansas City Charismatic Conference. Since that time, Mennonites have played a leading role in the general charismatic movement in the United States. When he passed away at 88 years of age in 1986, Bishop Nelson Litwiller had grown to be a respected elder statesman to younger leaders from many denominations.[14]

For the past decade, Mennonite Renewal Services has conducted scores of major renewal conferences in North America. These are well-attended and are making a major impact on the churches. In 1986 there were no fewer than fourteen regional conferences planned, some with thousands expected to attend.

The growth of the charismatic renewal among Mennonites has been spectacular. By 1985, estimates were that twenty percent of all Mennonites in the United States and Canada had received the baptism in the Holy Spirit, including both clergy and laity. In some conferences as many as thirty-five percent of the churches are active in the renewal. Many Mennonites believe with John Howard Yoder that Pentecostalism "is in our century the closest parallel to what Anabaptism was in the sixteenth."[15]

In recent years some local Mennonite churches have experienced spectacular growth through the power of the Holy Spirit. The most spectacular church growth in the Mennonite community has occurred recently in the Hopewell Mennonite Church in Pennsylvania. This congregation, under the leadership of charismatic pastor Merle Stoltzfus, has grown from fifty to 2,000 members in the past several years.[16]

Other success stories include the Trinity Church in Morton, Illinois, pastored by Mahlon Miller, and the English Lake Mennonite Church in North Judson, Indiana, led by pastor Arthur Good. These churches are also planting new congregations as an outreach of their local ministries.[17]

In retrospect, one could say that the experiences of the young vacation Bible school students in Strawberry Lake were not a temporary aberration but were in profound continuity with Mennonite faith and practice. By now, the renewal among Mennonites is one of the major success stories of the charismatic renewal.

A symbol of the acceptance of the renewal was the fact that in 1977 the Mennonite Church officially "restored" Gerald Derstine as an approved minister, thus ending twenty-two years of silence in the church.[18] His work has not been in vain. Today practically all the Mennonite missionaries of the world have received the baptism in the Holy Spirit and these mission fields are blazing areas of power evangelism. *Empowered*, the official magazine of Mennonite Renewal Services, now reports great outpourings of the Holy Spirit among Mennonites around the world.[19]

Mennonite charismatics are not content to rest on their laurels, however. Echoing the feelings of many in the renewal, Roy Koch says: "Although we are happy with what has been accomplished, there remains yet much more territory to be won."

For further information on the Mennonite Renewal write to:
Roy Koch
Mennonite Renewal Services
P.O. Box 722
Goshen, IN 46526

CHAPTER ELEVEN

The Methodist Renewal

In many ways, Methodism is the mother church for the hundreds of Holiness and Pentecostal denominations that have arisen in the past century. Founded in eighteenth-century England by John Wesley and his followers, Methodism arose as a renewal movement in the Church of England of which Wesley was a priest. Although Wesley remained an Anglican until his death, his Methodist Societies became separate denominations contrary to his wishes.

The name Methodist was given in derision to Wesley and his friends in the Holy Club at Oxford University in the 1720s. By following a method of prayer, confession and frequent communion, this group of university students attempted to fulfill the admonition of Hebrews 12:14: "Follow peace with all men, and holiness without which no man shall see the Lord."[1]

In seeking holiness, Wesley developed the theology of the second blessing of entire sanctification which could be received after conversion. Although he taught that sanctification was a process, Wesley also held out the possibility of an instantaneous experience similar to that of some great Catholic and Anglican mystics.

The idea of subsequence, that is, a second-blessing experience following conversion, is thus the basic theological principle of the Holiness and Pentecostal movements. Following Wesley, most of the Holiness churches, such as the Church of the Nazarene, have stressed the ethical cleansing aspect of the experience, while the Pentecostals, following Wesley's colleague, John Fletcher, have stressed the baptism in the Holy Spirit aspect with their own unique emphasis on accompanying manifestations of the charismata.[2]

Methodists in America

When Francis Asbury organized the American Methoist Church in Baltimore in 1784, he read Wesley's direction to the conference: "We believe that God's design in raising up the preachers called Methodists in America is to reform the continent and spread scriptural holiness over these lands." The nineteenth-century Methodists took Wesley seriously. They spread scriptural holiness over America by circuit rider preachers and by the camp meeting which became a Methodist specialty in frontier America.[3]

The frontier Methodists became famous also for their expressive worship and the demonstrations that often accompanied their revivals. Such exercises as "the jerks," "treeing the devil," being "slain in the Spirit," the "holy dance" and the "holy laugh" were not uncommon in these services. They were often laughingly called "Methodist fits." To the faithful, however, they were seen as signs of God's presence and power. Thus if people fell on the floor "slain by the Spirit" while a Methodist preacher ministered, it was considered the best sign that he was called to be a bishop.[4]

During these years, the Methodists grew by leaps and bounds in the United States. They spread from coast to coast and border to border. By the end of the Civil War, Methodists were accounted to be the largest denominational family in America.

As the church grew in numbers, wealth and influence, it became increasingly difficult to keep the second-blessing teaching alive and vital among both ministers and laymen. By 1839 a movement to breathe new life into the church and renew the experience of sanctification was begun by Phoebe and Walter Palmer in New York City. Working with Timothy Merritt and his *Guide to Holiness*, which was published in Boston, the Palmers led in teaching an altar terminology whereby one was sanctified instantaneously by placing his "all on the altar."[5]

Another renewal movement was inaugurated after the Civil War by New York Methodist pastors John Inskip and Alfred Cookman, at the suggestion of a laywoman from Pennsylvania, Harriett Drake. Through their efforts, the National Holiness Association was formed in Vineland, New Jersey, in 1867. This loose association soon grew to be a nationwide Holiness crusade that gathered huge crowds to old Methodist campgrounds to pray for a return of the old-time power. Although this effort was ecumenical, Methodist preachers and laypersons led the way.[6]

As this movement spread, two tendencies appeared. One was a turn to extreme legalism which caused a wedge between moderate Methodists and more radical Holiness teachers. Another trend was to speak of the second blessing as a baptism of the Holy Ghost for an enduement of power for service. Thus, the Methodist Church, which began as a renewal movement in Anglicanism, became itself the object of a renewal movement within its own ranks similar to Wesley's efforts a century earlier.[7]

By the twentieth century, however, the mainline Methodist churches in America largely rejected the Holiness renewal efforts as well as the frontier spiritual demonstrations that often accompanied Holiness preaching. The church then turned to an emphasis on education and social action. As a result, by the turn of the century, several dozen Holiness and Pentecostal denominations went their separate ways in order to emphasize the deeper life that they felt was being abandoned by the mainline Methodist churches.[8]

Tommy Tyson and the "Charismatic" Methodists

The story of Tommy Tyson is that of a twentieth-century Methodist pastor and evangelist who went back to the spiritual roots of his tradition in order to bring the power of the Holy Spirit back to his church. Coming from a family of Methodist preachers in North Carolina, Tyson had pastored several churches in the North Carolina conference when he felt a need for a deeper work of God in his life and ministry. In 1952, while serving as pastor of the Bethany Methodist Church in Durham, North Carolina, he was baptized in the Holy Spirit and experienced speaking in tongues.[9]

When he shared his new experience with his parishioners, they shied away from him. He then considered leaving the ministry and working as a layman. Going to his bishop, Paul Garber, he explained, "If no more than I have now is causing this kind of a reaction, there's no telling what will happen if the Lord really gets hold of me." Then he told him, "I am already packed."

The bishop's reply was a welcome relief and an open invitation to begin a charismatic ministry in the Methodist Church: "Now you just go back and unpack that bag. You're not going anyplace. We need you. We want you. But you need us too," said the bishop.

Two years later in 1954, Tyson was appointed as a conference evangelist and began a worldwide ministry of teaching and preaching which was instrumental in leading thousands of ministers and laymen into the Pentecostal experience. Although his ministry was especially influential in Methodist circles, he also became a leading speaker for Catholic and Episcopal charismatics.[10]

Through his ministry in Camps Farthest Out he spread the charismatic movement to thousands of others. In the middle 1960s, he became a close friend with Oral Roberts and served as the first director of religious life on the Oral Roberts University campus. His friendship with Roberts helped the charismatic movement to gain a more receptive attitude within the church.[11]

Other Methodist leaders followed Tyson at ORU and helped to bring the seminary into being. The leading influence in shaping the seminary was Jimmy Buskirk whom Roberts recruited from Emory University to serve as the founding dean of the graduate school of theology. Working closely with Buskirk was Bishop Mack Stokes, whose support and presence helped the institution gain credibility both in the academic world and in the United Methodist Church. Other "cradle" Methodists who worked at ORU and who were widely known as charismatics were Bob Stamps and Robert Tuttle.[12]

The "Adopted" Methodist Charismatics

Perhaps the most notable charismatic figure among Methodists is Oral Roberts, an "adopted" member of the church. Born in the home of Pentecostal Holiness preachers in eastern Oklahoma, Roberts became known worldwide in the 1950s for his tent divine healing crusades. During the time his ministry stirred controversy among his own Pentecostal brethren, Roberts was gaining respect in the traditional mainline churches because of his television ministry.[13]

In 1965, when he began his university in Tulsa, the charismatic movement was growing in the mainline churches. In time, Methodists grew to be a major source of the financial support for his ministry. Through the friendship of Finis Crutchfield, pastor of the Boston Avenue Methodist Church in Tulsa, Oklahoma, and Oklahoma bishop Angie Smith, Roberts joined the United Methodist Church in 1968. He was accepted as a local preacher although he vowed to continue preaching the same message he had proclaimed as a Pentecostal. After this, Oral Roberts University became a major training center for Methodist preachers.[14]

Another "adopted" Methodist charismatic leader was Ross Whetstone, who came to the church as an officer from the Salvation Army. Whetstone had been baptized in the Holy Ghost in 1937 as an 18-year-old boy. The next year, he joined the Salvation Army, where he was commissioned as an officer in 1939. In 1950 he transferred his ordination to the Central New York Conference of the Methodist Church.[15]

After pastoring several Methodist churches, Whetstone was called to provide leadership for the lay witness movement as an executive on the board of evangelism for the denomination. By the 1970s Whetstone was looked on as the leading spokesman for Methodist charismatics and was given increasing responsibility for overseeing the movement in the church. Over the years, hundreds of other Holiness and Pentecostal ministers have transferred to the Methodist Church and have carried on forceful Spirit-filled ministries in their assignments. They, like Roberts and Whetstone, have been a leavening influence in the church.[16]

United Methodist Renewal Fellowship

Although Tyson and others had led thousands of Methodists into a Pentecostal experience, a charismatic Methodist organization did not exist until 1977 when Whetstone and others joined other denominations in organizing the Kansas City Charismatic Conference. In Kansas City the Methodist delegation formed the United Methodist Renewal Services Fellowship to serve as a central rallying force for Methodist charismatics.

In 1980 the UMRSF was given offices in the national headquarters of the United Methodist Church in Nashville, Tennessee. Rather than being another adversary pressure group within the church, the UMRSF is officially recognized by the board of discipleship and enjoys the support of the church at large. An indication of this acceptance is the fact that the board of discipleship charged this group to represent the interests of the United Methodist Church at the New Orleans Congresses on the Holy Spirit in 1986 and 1987.[17]

The UMRSF sponsors many conferences and seminars around the country in its efforts to renew the church. The major annual gatherings are the Aldersgate Conferences on the Holy Spirit, which gather some 2,000 to 3,000 participants annually. The group also publishes a newsletter entitled *Manna* to keep the members and friends of the Methodist charismatic renewal movement informed.[18]

The theology of the Methodist charismatic movement is similar to that of other mainline Protestant charismatic movements. While not emphasizing the instant second-blessing sanctification teachings of the classical Holiness bodies and the initial evidence doctrine of the classical Pentecostals, the Methodist charismatics see baptism in the Holy Spirit as the actualization of the Holy Spirit and His gifts that were received at initiation. They do stress, however, the continuing manifestation of all the gifts of the Spirit in the ongoing life of the believer and the church.

Despite the Methodist roots of the Pentecostal movement, the American Methodist Church was late in issuing a report on the charismatic movement. When it was issued in 1976, the report pointed to Wesley's mature teaching on the progressive aspect of sanctification and indicated that Methodist charismatics who take over classical Pentecostal theology "are no longer Methodists, at least in the Wesleyan sense."[19]

The Methodist Church might well be called the mother of denominations because of the many schisms resulting in the formation of new bodies. Among the casualties of the past are such Holiness churches with Methodist roots as the Church of the Nazarene, the Free Methodist Church, the Wesleyan Church and the Salvation Army. Many of these bodies adopted doctrinal statements and church structures almost identical with classical Methodist usages.

The Methodists also contributed much to the formation of the classical Pentecostal denominations. The theological foundations of Pentecostalism were laid by former Methodists such as Charles Parham, William J. Seymour and J.H. King. The basic theology of almost all Pentecostal bodies in the world is essentially the Arminian perfectionistic theology of Methodism with some charismatic and dispensational additions.

Perhaps the most striking event in Methodist charismatic history was the schism in Chile in 1909 which produced the Pentecostal Methodist Church of Chile. Under the leadership of Willis Hoover, an American missionary, a Pentecostal revival broke out in the Methodist churches in Valparaiso and Santiago where simple church members spoke in tongues, prophesied and "danced in the Spirit." In a short time thirty-seven Pentecostals were tried in a church court for being "irrational and anti-Methodist." At the time there were 6,000 Methodists in Chile. The Pentecostals organized the Iglesia Metodista Pentecostal (Pentecostal Methodist Church) later that year.[20]

Today the Pentecostals in Chile number almost two million while the Methodist church that conducted the trial has dwindled to fewer than 5,000 members. The Evangelical Cathedral of Chile is the Jotabeche Methodist Pentecostal congregation of Santiago which now numbers 150,000 members. For many years this was the largest Protestant church in the world.[21]

The Pentecostal Methodists of Chile claim to be the true spiritual heirs of Wesley and accuse the Episcopal Methodists of wandering off into leftist Marxist theology. A similar division in Brazil took place in 1965 when the charismatic Methodists organized the Wesleyan Methodist Church of Brazil as a classical Pentecostal body. Today this growing movement has over 50,000 members and adherents in Brazil.

Now there seems to be a more tolerant spirit arising among many Methodists in regard to renewal movements. The basic liberal orientation of United Methodist leadership opens the door to the existence of a wide variety of movements within the church. Charismatics are tolerated and even encouraged as an example of the freedom and pluralism that exist in the denomination.

With this attitude, it may be possible for the 1.7 million American Methodists who identify with the charismatic movement to remain in the church and carry out a significant ministry of renewal. Also there may be a growing tendency among Methodist leaders to begin conversations with the "children" of Methodism who have shown more vigorous growth than the mother church.

The Methodist Charismatic Movement Today

Across America many Methodist congregations are involved in charismatic renewal. In most cases they have the cooperation and support of their bishops, although in some areas charismatic pastors have difficulty with their ecclesiastical superiors.

By 1986, the United Methodist Church was moving to integrate the renewal into the structures of the church. Avenues of communication were created by the appointment of charismatic jurisdictional coordinators for the five jurisdictions in the United States. Plans were also made for other consultants and coordinators to be appointed to work with these jurisdictional leaders in interpreting the renewal to the bishops and integrating its dynamic force into the life of the church.[22]

Among the leading pastors and congregations involved

in the renewal are First United Methodist Church, Tulsa, Oklahoma, Jimmy Buskirk, pastor; First United Methodist Church, Bedford, Texas, Lee A. Bedford, pastor; Aldersgate United Methodist Church, College Station, Texas, Terry Teykl, pastor; Bayshore United Methodist Church, Tampa, Florida, Frank Segars, pastor; and St. Mark's United Methodist Church in Anaheim, California, David Walker, pastor. And there are many others, according to Whetstone.

For further information, contact:
Ross Whetstone
United Methodist Renewal Services Fellowship
P.O. Box 50086
Nashville, TN 37205-0086
(615) 340-7326

CHAPTER TWELVE

The Orthodox Renewal

The Eastern Orthodox Church constitutes the second largest family of Christians in the world, numbering some 168 million members worldwide in 1985. Over sixty million of these are members of the Russian Orthodox Church in the Soviet Union and live under conditions of repression and ongoing persecution. In Greece, nearly nine million people embrace the Orthodox faith—98.1 percent of the total population of that country. Millions more live in other Eastern European and Middle Eastern nations dominated by communism and Islam. For centuries, Orthodoxy has been a martyr church, with millions of her faithful slain for professing faith in Christ (it is estimated that over thirty million Orthodox Christians were martyred from 1917 to 1953 in Russia alone). They have kept their faith in Jesus when their own country became for them a foreign land.[1]

Here in America, the Orthodox Church claims some five million members. These are distributed among a number of jurisdictions: Greek, Russian, Antiochian,

Ukrainian and several others. In 1965, the Orthodox Church in America (OCA) was formed as a self-governing entity with the blessings of the Russian bishops. It now claims one million English-speaking members. Orthodoxy in America is rapidly moving from its initial status as an immigrant church to hold a distinct place in American religious life.

Orthodoxy has always claimed to be charismatic in its worship and piety. At no time has it held to a theory of the cessation of the gifts of the Holy Spirit. Signs and wonders, including prophecy, healing and miracles, have traditionally been accepted as part of the heritage of the church.[2]

Despite this tradition, no major body of Christians in the world has been less affected by the charismatic movement of recent decades. Even so, against the resistance of many church leaders, several Orthodox priests and laymen have persistently struggled to plant the seeds of renewal.

Eusebius A. Stephanou

An early leader of this charismatic renewal in the Orthodox Church was Eusebius A. Stephanou, of Fort Wayne, Indiana. Stephanou, a celibate priest descended from a long line of Orthodox clergymen, brought impressive credentials to his task of charismatic leadership. Educated at the University of Michigan, Holy Cross School of Theology and the General Episcopal Seminary in New York, he holds the B.A., S.T.M. and Th.D. degrees. He was a professor of theology and sub-dean at Holy Cross and subsequently held a teaching post at Notre Dame University.[3]

In 1968, feeling a need to "bring the Orthodox Church into line with the gospel of Christ," Stephanou launched a magazine entitled *The Logos*. His goal was the "re-evangelization of our people." Stephanou's criticism of the Greek Orthodox hierarchy, however, quickly got him into trouble, and he was suspended from the priesthood for six months for "undermining church authority." For the next several years, Stephanou, his magazine and his insistent calls for reform, proved to be a source of controversy within the Orthodox Church.

In 1972, Stephanou encountered another Orthodox priest, Athanasius Emmert of Huntington, West Virginia, who shared with him about the life-changing power of the Holy Spirit.[4] Emmert laid hands on Stephanou and prayed for the "release" of the Holy Spirit (Orthodox Christians pray to be filled with the Holy Spirit when they are baptized—usually as infants— and look at the charismatic experience as a release of that gift already received). He was filled with the power of God, began to speak in other tongues and thereby changed *The Logos* into an instrument for serving charismatic renewal in the Orthodox Church.[5]

Orthodox Charismatic Renewal

The following year, the very first Orthodox Charismatic Conference was held in Ann Arbor, Michigan, with about 100 people in attendance. At that time there were estimated to be 1,000 Orthodox charismatics scattered among two dozen prayer groups. Stephanou, Emmert and a number of other clergy and laymen continued to work for renewal through the Logos Ministry for Orthodox Renewal.

Because of his renewal leadership, criticism of the Orthodox hierarchy and continued reform activism, Stephanou has suffered several disciplinary actions. In July 1983 he was censured by his bishop and archbishop and placed on indefinite suspension despite hundreds of letters of support from his charismatic friends in the Orthodox Church. The final outcome of this action is still unresolved. Stephanou continues as editor of *The Logos* and is a popular speaker at charismatic conferences in America and abroad.[6]

In 1977, another Orthodox charismatic ministry emerged on the scene: the Service Committee for Orthodox Charismatic Renewal. This committee sought to bring together charismatic leaders from a wide variety of Orthodox jurisdictions to facilitate administration, coordination and communication in the movement. They have sponsored a number of renewal conferences throughout the United States and Canada and publish a monthly newsletter, *Theosis*. Boris Zabrodsky, a Ukrainian Orthodox priest from Chicago, Illinois, is president of the Service Committee. Serving with Zabrodsky is Gerald Munk of Lansing, Michigan, the editor of *Theosis*. Munk also served on the steering committee planning the New Orleans Congresses on the Holy Spirit and World Evangelization in 1986 and 1987.[7]

Charismatic renewal continues to grow among Orthodox Christians in the United States. In 1986, leaders estimated that some 12,000 Orthodox were active in charismatic renewal in America with many thousands more in other nations.

For further information on charismatic renewal in the Orthodox Church, write to:
Gerald Munk
Theosis Newsletter
P.O. Box 4277

The Orthodox Renewal

Eusebius A. Stephanou
The Logos
2133 Embassy Drive
Fort Wayne, IN 46816

CHAPTER THIRTEEN

The Pentecostal Holiness Church

The Pentecostal Holiness Church was organized as a Holiness denomination several years before the Pentecostal movement began in the United States. Its roots lie in the National Holiness Association movement which began in Vineland, New Jersey, in 1867 just after the end of the Civil War. The present church represents the merger of three bodies which were products of that movement.

Founded by Ambrose B. Crumpler, a Methodist Holiness preacher from North Carolina, the church was organized in 1896 as the North Carolina Holiness Association. The name was changed to the Pentecostal Holiness Church when the first congregation was formed in Greensboro, North Carolina, in 1898.

The other major group that flowed into the present denomination was the Fire-Baptized Holiness Church founded in Iowa in 1895 by Benjamin H. Irwin, a former Baptist preacher. This group taught a third blessing after sanctification called the baptism in the Holy Ghost and fire. By 1898, this group had organized a national denomination with churches in eight states and two Canadian provinces.

The Fire-Baptized movement almost disappeared in 1900 after Irwin backslid and abandoned the church. Before this he had taught several more baptisms including the baptisms of "dynamite," "liddite" and "oxidite."[1]

The Churches Become Pentecostal

The 1906 annual conference of the Pentecostal Holiness Church of North Carolina was notable for the absence of Gaston B. Cashwell, one of the leading evangelists and pastors in the new denomination since he left Methodism to join the new church in 1903. Crumpler, the leader of the conference, read a letter from Cashwell that greatly interested the delegates. In it he asked forgiveness from anyone he had offended and announced that he was going to Los Angeles "to seek for the baptism of the Holy Ghost."[2]

For several months there had been great interest in the Azusa Street revival throughout the South because of the glowing eyewitness accounts by Frank Bartleman in the *Way of Faith*, a regional Holiness magazine. Cashwell was the only minister venturesome enough to take action. He decided to make the long journey to Los Angeles to find out for himself if this was indeed the new Pentecost they had been praying for and expecting for years. Trusting God to supply his needs, he bought a one-way train ticket to Los Angeles and traveled in the only suit he owned.

Once in Los Angeles, Cashwell went directly to the Azusa Street Mission. He was dismayed at what he saw. The pastor, William J. Seymour, was a black man, as were most of the worshippers. When blacks laid hands upon him to receive the baptism, he abruptly left the meeting confused and disappointed. That night, however, God dealt with his racial prejudices and gave him a love for blacks and a renewed hunger to be baptized in the Holy Spirit. The next night, at Cashwell's request, Seymour and several young blacks laid hands again on this Southern gentleman, who was baptized in the Spirit and, according to his own account, spoke perfect German. Before Cashwell returned to North Carolina, Seymour and the Azusa faithful took up an offering and presented him with a new suit and enough money for the return journey.[3]

The Flame Spreads

Upon arriving in his hometown of Dunn, North Carolina, in December 1906, Cashwell immediately preached Pentecost in the local Holiness church. Interest was so great that in the first week of January 1907 he rented a three-story tobacco warehouse near the railroad tracks in Dunn for a month-long Pentecostal crusade, which became for the East Coast another Azusa Street.

Most of the ministers in the three largest area Holiness movements came by the scores hungry to receive their own "personal Pentecost." These churches included the Pentecostal Holiness Church, the Fire-Baptized Holiness Church and the Holiness Freewill Baptist Churches of the area. Overnight most of the ministers and churches in these groups were swept "lock, stock and barrel" into the Pentecostal movement.

A month later, the Fire-Baptized Holiness Church general overseer Joseph H. King invited Cashwell to preach at his church in Toccoa, Georgia. Although King had heard of the new baptism accompanied by glossolalia, he was not fully convinced of its validity. Upon hearing one message from Cashwell, he knelt at the altar and received the baptism "in a quiet but powerful manifestation of tongues."[4]

In the next six months Cashwell completed a whirl-wind preaching tour of the Southern states which established him as the "apostle of Pentecost to the South." On a trip to Birmingham, Alabama, in the summer of 1907 he brought the message of Pentecost to A.J. Tomlinson, general overseer of the Church of God in Cleveland, Tennessee, and to H.G. Rodgers and M.M. Pinson, later founders of the Assemblies of God.[5]

The Church Officially Becomes Pentecostal

Though the Pentecostal experience was sweeping his church, Crumpler was one of the few who refused to countenance the theory of "initial evidence." Although he accepted the validity of tongues, he did not believe that everyone had to speak in tongues to experience a genuine baptism in the Holy Spirit. For several months Crumpler and the Pentecostal party led by Cashwell and his converts struggled over the issue.

The issue came to a head in the annual conference which met in Dunn, North Carolina, in November 1908. About ninety percent of the ministers and laity had experienced tongues by this time. On the first day of the convention, delegates re-elected Crumpler as president, but the "initial evidence" battle had come to a head. The next day he left forever the convention and the church he had founded. The Pentecostals had won.

The convention immediately added a Pentecostal article to the statement of faith which accepted tongues as the initial evidence. As far as is known, this was the first church body to adopt a Pentecostal statement as the official doctrine of the denomination.

Delegates also selected *The Bridegroom's Messenger*,

a magazine published by Cashwell, as the official periodical of the church. A final action was taken in 1909 when the word Pentecostal was once again added to the name of the church. It had been dropped in 1903 in an attempt to identify the church further with the Holiness movement.[6]

Another citadel to accept Pentecostalism was the Bible college in Greenville, South Carolina, founded by Nickles J. Holmes in 1898 as a Holiness school. In 1907, Holmes and most of his faculty had received the Pentecostal experience and had spoken in tongues under Cashwell's influence. By 1909, Holmes accepted Pentecostalism and subsequently his school became an early theological and educational center for the movement. Now officially related to the Pentecostal Holiness Church, Holmes College of the Bible stands as the oldest continuing Pentecostal educational institution in the world.[7]

Mergers

By the end of 1908, much of the Southern Holiness movement had entered the Pentecostal fold. In the following months, a feeling emerged that those of "like precious faith" should unite to promote the Pentecostal message more effectively. This led to a merger of the Pentecostal Holiness Church with the Fire-Baptized Holiness Church in 1911 in the camp meeting village of Falcon, North Carolina. The same ecumenical feeling led to the merger of the churches affiliated with the college in 1915. These congregations were located mostly in South Carolina and had roots in the Presbyterian Church.[8]

The Theology of the Church

Pentecostal Holiness doctrine has roots in the original

teachings of the Azusa Street revival. Already a Holiness church before 1906, it taught the Wesleyan theology of instant second-blessing sanctification. After Azusa Street, the church simply added the baptism in the Holy Spirit evidenced by tongues as a third blessing. This was in harmony with the teachings of Irwin and the Fire-Baptized branch of the church.

Since 1908, the Pentecostal Holiness Church has taught what are known as five cardinal doctrines, that is, justification by faith, entire sanctification, the baptism in the Holy Spirit evidenced by speaking in tongues, Christ's atonement providing for divine healing, and the imminent, premillennial second coming of Christ.

Influential books in forming this theology were G.F. Taylor's 1907 book *The Spirit and the Bride* and J.H. King's 1911 volume, *From Passover to Pentecost.*[9]

Over the years the church has gained a reputation for its defense of what its leaders consider the original Pentecostal message. In the "finished work" controversy over sanctification after 1910, the church roundly defended the second work of entire sanctification against the teachings of William Durham. Those who accepted Durham's teachings eventually formed the Assemblies of God in 1914.[10]

The only schism in the church's history came in 1920 when a division came over divine healing and the use of medicine. Some Georgia pastors defended the right of Christians to use medicine and doctors, while most of the church leaders taught that one should trust God for healing without recourse to medicine. Those who advocated the use of medicine withdrew from the denomination to form the Congregational Holiness Church in 1921.[11]

Growing Pains

In the post-World War II era, the Pentecostal Holiness Church along with other American Pentecostal bodies experienced tremendous growth. Much of this came during the era of the "divine healing" crusades of the late 1940s and early 1950s. Leading this movement was Oral Roberts, a Pentecostal Holiness evangelist from Oklahoma. At first immensely popular with most Pentecostal laymen and church leaders, Roberts' ministry became increasingly controversial after 1953.

For a decade the church was torn by pro- and anti-Roberts factions with some anti-Roberts ministers calling for a schism in the church. In the end, cooler heads prevailed and the threat of division passed. In time leading churchmen such as R.O. Corvin and Bishop Oscar Moore worked with Roberts in his evangelistic association and in his new university.

By the mid-1960s Roberts had won the support of most of his denomination, including Bishop Joseph A. Synan. Synan, an early Roberts opponent, joined in the dedication of Oral Roberts University in 1967. Despite his acceptance, Roberts joined the Methodist Church in 1968 to the dismay and puzzlement of his many friends in all the Pentecostal denominations.[12]

The Roberts story illustrates a significant fact about the denomination: The Pentecostal Holiness Church is as famous for the ministers who have left the church as for those who have remained. In addition to Roberts, such leaders as Charles Stanley, former president of the Southern Baptist Convention, and C.M. Ward, former Assemblies of God radio preacher, were born and spiritually formed in the Pentecostal Holiness Church. Others in this category are T.L. Lowery of the Church of God and Dan Sheaffer of the Assemblies of God.

Pentecostal Ecumenism

For many decades there was little contact between the various American Pentecostal bodies except by ministers who transferred from one denomination to another. However, there were cases of proselytism and "sheep stealing" that caused unpleasant feelings between the various groups. This began to change during the dark days of World War II when the first steps were taken to bring Pentecostals into fellowship with each other.

The first contacts were made in 1943 in the lobbies of the newly formed National Association of Evangelicals. Several Pentecostal bodies served as charter members of this group which was drawn together by the emergency situation brought about by the war. The Pentecostal Holiness Church was one of these groups.

By 1948, several Pentecostal groups formed the Pentecostal Fellowship of North America in Des Moines, Iowa. Preliminary to this organization was a rally in Washington, D.C., where plans for a constitution were formulated. Leading figures in this meeting were Bishop Synan, who helped formulate the constitution, and Oral Roberts who preached in the final public rally. From those early days, the Pentecostal Holiness Church has taken a leading role in the PFNA meetings as well as the World Pentecostal Conferences that have met every three years since 1947.[13]

The Church Today

In the 1960s the Pentecostal Holiness Church began to branch out beyond the United States by affiliating with sister Pentecostal bodies in the Third World. This was done in addition to its traditional world mission efforts. In 1967 an affiliation was formed with the

Pentecostal Methodist Church of Chile, one of the largest national Pentecostal churches in the world. At the time, the Jotabeche Pentecostal Methodist congregation was the largest church in the world with over 60,000 members.

Today this congregation is in second place despite the fact that it has grown to number 150,000 members. In 1985 the Pentecostal Methodist Church of Chile claimed no less than 1.2 million members and adherents.

A similar affiliation was forged with the Wesleyan Methodist Church of Brazil in 1985. A neo-Pentecostal body with roots in the Brazilian Methodist Church, the Wesleyan Church numbered some 50,000 members and adherents in 1985.[14]

With 120,000 adult baptized members in the United States and mission churches and affiliates in thirty-five nations, the Pentecostal Holiness Church in 1986 numbered 1.6 million persons around the world.

Leading the church since 1981 is Bishop Leon Stewart of Alabama. Stewart is unique in that, despite the fact that he is legally blind, he was chosen by the general conference to lead his denomination. The church headquarters since 1974 has been located in Oklahoma City where the denomination has more congregations than any other city in the world.

The largest Pentecostal Holiness churches in the United States include Northwood Temple in Fayetteville, North Carolina, pastored by John Hedgepeth; Evangelistic Temple in Tulsa, Oklahoma, pastored by Dan Beller; Christian Heritage Church in Tallahassee, Florida, pastored by Bob Shelley; World Agape Korean Church in Los Angeles, pastored by Jon Kim; and Calvary Chapel in San Jose, California, pastored by Dan Greenlee.

The leadership of the church is looking toward the last years of the century as the time of the greatest growth and evangelization in its history. In 1985 a program known as Target 2000 was launched. The goal of this program is for the church to be able to claim one-tenth of one percent of the world population for Jesus Christ by the end of the century. This would mean a church of 6.5 million members by the year 2000. To achieve this goal, new churches are being opened in world class cities in the United States and other nations each year.[15]

For many decades the Pentecostal Holiness Church was a church that spoke with a Southern accent and was largely a rural denomination ministering in the South and the Midwest. It now wishes to minister and preach the gospel in all the languages and accents of the world.

For more information contact:
  Office of Public Relations
  The International Pentecostal Holiness Church
  P.O. Box 12609
  Oklahoma City, OK 73157
  (405) 787-7110

CHAPTER FOURTEEN

The Presbyterian and Reformed Renewal

From their earliest days in Switzerland and Scotland, the Presbyterians have been rock-ribbed proponents of John Calvin's theology, a system known for its tight presbyterian ecclesiology as well as its more famous theological propositions. The presbyterian system that has developed since the sixteenth century has not been known for innovation and experimentation, but rather for adherence to the strict formulations of its founding father.

It might come as a surprise to many to find that there is a rich and even pioneering history of renewal in the Presbyterian churches. Although Calvin, along with Luther, subscribed to the cessation theory of the charismata, to Calvin it was not because God withdrew these gifts from the church. In his *Institutes*, Calvin explained that they fell into disuse in the churches because of "a lack of faith." He never forbade their use in the churches nor felt that they should be forbidden. Moreover, because of his extended attention to the Third Person of the Trinity in his writings, he has been called "the theologian of the Holy Spirit" among the reformers.[1]

Because of the work of the Princeton Presbyterian theologians B.B. Warfield and Charles Hodge, some twentieth-century Presbyterians have been noted for a fundamentalist position that excludes both perfectionism and Pentecostalism from the Calvinist tradition. The standard work on the subject was Warfield's stern *Counterfeit Miracles*, a 1918 book which denied that any genuine miracles have occurred in the world since the age of the apostles. Another book in this genre was Ronald Knox's *Enthusiasm*, which took a dim view of all emotionalism in religion.[2]

Despite this strain of thought among some Presbyterians, many American pastors have participated and even pioneered in spiritual renewal in a way that would have displeased Warfield, but would perhaps have been applauded by Calvin. Britain and America have been the setting for many of these spiritual pioneers.

Early Presbyterian Revivalists

In 1800 one of the greatest revivals in American history broke out at Cane Ridge, Kentucky, under the leadership of three Presbyterian ministers: James McGready, William Hodges and John Rankin. Eyewitnesses reported that the floors of the Red River Presbyterian Church were "covered with the slain" while others cried loudly for mercy. At times the pastors would "dance before the Lord" declaring "this is the Holy Ghost." Soon as many as 25,000 gathered in the forests to praise the Lord. This began the great camp meeting tradition in America. The effects of the revival were nationwide.[3]

These demonstrations were not new in American

religion. They had all been seen in the 1700s in the revival services of Jonathan Edwards, that great Calvinist theologian and pastor from Northhampton, Massachusetts. It was not unusual for sinners to scream out for mercy or fall out in the aisles under the conviction of the Holy Spirit. Though Edwards was a Puritan minister of the Congregational Church, he stood in the Calvinist tradition of the Presbyterians.[4]

One of the major spiritual movements among American Presbyterians also occurred on the frontier in the years between 1810 and 1840. The major cause of a split between eastern and western Presbyterians was a disagreement over educational requirements for ordination. Because of great revivals and spiritual manifestations, large numbers of converts joined the churches. This led to a lack of ministers. Traditionally Presbyterians had insisted on a seminary degree for entry into the ministry. The Westerners felt that those with less education could also qualify to minister to the masses of new converts.

Because of the educational question and the manifestation of such spiritual gifts as tongues and healing, and the manifestations of spiritual joy, the Cumberland Presbyterian Church was formed in 1810 as a separate denomination. It has continued its revivalistic tradition in the mid-South until this day.

Presbyterians also took a leading part in the great Holiness revivals that swept America in the middle and late 1800s. For instance, in 1859, William Boardman wrote a book entitled *The Higher Christian Life*, which interpreted the Methodist teaching on entire sanctification to those in the Presbyterian and Reformed tradition. A former Presbyterian, Charles Grandison Finney, became the greatest revivalist of his day after receiving a vivid experience in the Holy Spirit that radically changed his life and ministry. His powerful evangelistic ministry marked Finney as the first "professional evangelist" in America.[5]

A Presbyterian pastor actually led the first charismatic renewal movement of modern times to penetrate a mainline denomination. He was Edward Irving, who led a gifts movement in the Regent's Square Presbyterian Church in London in 1831. After a woman lay leader, Mary Campbell, spoke in tongues and prophesied, Irving was tried by his presbytery and defrocked. Since the English Presbyterian Church refused to countenance these extra-ordinary gifts in their sanctuaries, Irving aided in the beginnings of the Catholic Apostolic Church which existed until 1901. Although he never spoke in tongues and died soon after the inauguration of the new movement, Irving will always be remembered as an early persecuted pioneer of Pentecostalism among Presbyterians.[6]

Some years later in America, A.B. Simpson, a Canadian-born Presbyterian pastor from New York City, began to teach the possibility of divine healing in answer to prayer. This came after he was instantly healed of a long-standing condition. He also accepted the basic teachings of the Holiness movement and received a sanctification experience in 1881. At about the same time, he experienced a tremendous call to send missionaries around the world. After some fifteen years as a Presbyterian pastor, he began an interdenominational agency which he called the Christian and Missionary Alliance in 1886.

Simpson's Alliance soon developed into a separate

denomination which sent large numbers of missionaries to many nations of the world. His school at Nyack, New York, became an outstanding institution for training missionaries. In 1907, the school in Nyack experienced a Pentecostal outpouring that almost brought the Alliance into the Pentecostal movement. Later, in 1914, several former Alliance ministers were instrumental in founding the Assemblies of God.

Another Presbyterian pioneer in this era was N.J. Holmes, pastor of the Second Presbyterian Church in Greenville, South Carolina. In 1896, Holmes journeyed to Northfield, Massachusetts, to attend a "higher life" conference led by D.L. Moody, who had earlier received a powerful baptism in the Holy Spirit. In Moody's meeting Holmes received an experience in the Holy Spirit which he later identified with the Wesleyan experience of entire sanctification. In 1898 he began his school on Paris Mountain outside Greenville. By this time, Holmes had been tried and expelled from the Enoree Presbytery for espousing the new experience and theology.

In 1905, a student in Holmes' school, Lida Purkie, electrified the student body when she spoke in tongues in a prayer meeting. A year later, the entire school, including both faculty and student body, received their personal Pentecost. This revival occurred after Holmes heard the Pentecostal message from G.B. Cashwell who had visited Azusa Street a few months earlier. Holmes College of the Bible, the oldest college in the Pentecostal world, continues as a faith school related to the Pentecostal Holiness Church. Several of the earliest congregations in that denomination were first known as Brewerton Presbyterian Churches.[7]

Presbyterian Charismatics

When the neo-Pentecostal or charismatic movement began in the mainline churches in the United States after World War II, the Presbyterians were again in the forefront of renewal. The first well-known Presbyterian pastor to experience tongues and healing and remain in his church was James Brown, pastor of the Upper Octorara Presbyterian congregation near Parkesburg just outside Philadelphia, Pennsylvania. In the mid-1950s Brown was baptized with the Holy Spirit and began to speak in tongues. This experience helped move him from an extremely liberal theological position to that of an evangelical charismatic Christian.

At first Brown was convinced that he could not remain a Presbyterian with his new experience. Perplexed as to what course of action he should follow, Brown asked David du Plessis for advice. "Stay in your church and renew it" was the word from the famous Pentecostal leader. This Brown determined to do.

His basic decision was to conduct traditional Presbyterian worship in the regular Sunday services, but to have neo-Pentecostal worship in informal Saturday evening sessions in the sanctuary. This strategy worked for over twenty years with a minimum of friction. In time the Saturday services attracted hundreds of enthusiastic worshippers each week with the little country church jammed with as many as 750 worshippers. Thousands of both clergy and laity were baptized in the Holy Spirit in these services. With Brown playing the tambourines, the services were joyful and full of praise. People from all denominations came to witness prophecy, tongues, interpretation and prayer for the sick. All along, Brown was active and accepted in his presbytery.[8]

These events were taking place in the late 1950s before the more famous events in Van Nuys, California, surrounding the ministry of Dennis Bennett. For several years prior to 1960, Brown had the largest charismatic prayer meeting in the United States. In 1977, he retired after thirty-seven years in the same pastorate, an early success story of the renewal movement.

Brick Bradford

The path of the Presbyterian spiritual pioneers became harder after the national news furor created by the Bennett case in California. The Presbyterians became litigious and defensive when Pentecostal phenomena appeared in their midst. An early casualty of a stiffening opposition in the church was George C. "Brick" Bradford, pastor of the First Presbyterian Church, El Reno, near Oklahoma City. Bradford was baptized in the Holy Spirit in 1966 at a CFO ("Camp Farthest Out") meeting in Ardmore, Oklahoma. As he was empowered by the Holy Spirit, Bradford said his "ministry was revolutionized."

When the leaders of the presbytery heard that Bradford was speaking in tongues, they immediately assumed that he needed mental counseling. Accordingly, he was sent to a psychiatrist who had also been filled with the Spirit. He gave Bradford a clean bill of health. Not satisfied with this result, the Washita presbytery sent him to another psychologist who gave them the diagnosis they desired. Despite the fact that he had been a lawyer and held a law degree from the University of Texas, Bradford was removed from his pastorate in December 1967.[9]

After this decision, Bradford retained his Presbyterian ordination for three more years and began an itinerant ministry speaking in whatever Presbyterian churches would open their doors. He also spoke in many Full Gospel Business Men's gatherings and Pentecostal churches. Freewill offerings supported his family during these lean years.

In May 1966, Bradford and five other Presbyterian charismatic ministers took an important step. They organized the Charismatic Communion which later took the name Presbyterian Charismatic Communion. This was the first charismatic organization to be formed in a mainline denomination. Bradford was chosen as the general secretary, a position he holds today. In one year, the new group had 125 Presbyterian ministers on its rolls, and in a short time hundreds of pastors and laymen joined forces in this well-organized ministry.[10]

The Robert Whitaker Case

Not long after this move, Bradford and the PCC were confronted with a landmark case which tested the place of the gifts of the Spirit in the Presbyterian system. This case arose because of a dispute concerning the ministry of Robert C. Whitaker, pastor of the Chandler Presbyterian Church near Phoenix, Arizona.

In 1962, Whitaker had been baptized in the Holy Spirit and had seen the Holy Spirit slowly but surely revolutionize his ministry and the ministry of the Chandler church. By 1967 a number of his members had spoken in tongues. Also, like James Brown, no tongues or laying on of hands was practiced in the regular services of the church. However, in home prayer meetings revival broke out. The church experienced tremendous growth in a short time, with most of the congregation in full support of the movement.

In 1967 a small group of dissenting elders was able

to persuade the presbytery of Phoenix to appoint an administrative commission to investigate Whitaker's ministry and the use of the gifts of the Holy Spirit within the life of the congregation. When Whitaker refused to take a vow to "cease and desist" from speaking in tongues, praying for the sick and casting out demons, the presbytery removed him as pastor of First Presbyterian Church in Chandler. Rather than accept this decision, he decided to appeal to the synod of Arizona on grounds that the verdict was contrary to Scripture and violated his conscience according to provisions within the Book of Order.[11]

In February 1968, when the appeal from the presbytery of Phoenix to the synod of Arizona failed, Whitaker was faced with accepting or appealing the decision. Giving strong counsel and aid to Whitaker was a leading figure in world Presbyterianism, the late John A. Mackay, president emeritus of Princeton Theological Seminary. Both Mackay and Bradford strongly encouraged Whitaker to continue the fight. Providentially, Bradford had been a lawyer before entering the ministry and offered his services as counsel for the plaintiff.

Bradford added a third reason for appealing to the Permanent Judicial Commission of the General Assembly, the highest court of the United Presbyterian Church. He argued that no lower judicatory (presbytery or synod) could add further vows to the ordination vows already set forth in the church constitution. In May 1968, *The Rev. Robert C. Whitaker vs. The Synod of Arizona* was decided in favor of Whitaker.[12]

It was a great moral victory for all charismatics in the mainline churches. But the victory did not end with the successful appeal. As a result of the Whitaker case, every Presbyterian minister was protected from arbitrary removal from his or her parish by a presbytery on grounds of involvement in the charismatic renewal. Because the case did not rule on the theological implications involved in the controversy, the 180th General Assembly (1968) ordered a theological study to be made on the question of tongues, healing, exorcism and the neo-Pentecostal movement in general.

The study commissioned by the general assembly was the first and possibly the most thorough one ever done by a major denomination. The members of the commission were made up of persons versed in theology, psychology, psychiatry, pastoral ministry and ecclesiology. The report was so groundbreaking and comprehensive that it served as a model for many other denominational reports in following years. Again, the Presbyterians were pioneers in renewal.

The report of those competent in the behavioral sciences "found no evidence of pathology in the movement." The exegetical sections of the report, while rejecting a separate experience of Holy Spirit baptism, did allow for the exercise of spiritual gifts in the contemporary church as long as they did not lead to disorder and division. Rejecting the cessation of the charismata theory, the report said: "We therefore conclude on the basis of Scripture, that the practice of glossolalia should neither be despised nor forbidden; on the other hand, it should not be emphasized nor made normative for Christian experience."

A set of guidelines was offered for both charismatics and non-charismatics, with a view toward keeping peace in the churches. Over all, the report was positive in its exegetical, psychological and pastoral sections. The report's guidelines were adopted overwhelmingly and the report as a whole was received by the 182nd General Assembly of the United Presbyterian Church in 1970 and has been the official policy of the church since that time.[13]

Despite this victory, other Presbyterian pastors faced legal difficulties in the churches in the years after 1970. Another classic case was that of Earl W. Morey Jr., pastor of the St. Giles Presbyterian Church of Richmond, Virginia, who was investigated and exonerated three times before the Hanover presbytery would accept his right to exercise the gifts of the Spirit in the prayer meetings of the church.

Recent Growth and Development

None of these legal obstacles, however, could hinder the work of the Holy Spirit in the American Presbyterian churches. Throughout the 1970s the renewal moved with ever-increasing force in the churches. In Hollywood's First Presbyterian Church, one of the largest Presbyterian churches in the world, over 600 members were said to be speaking in tongues. Other prominent Presbyterian leaders including Louis Evans of the National Presbyterian Church in Washington, D.C., his wife, Colleen Townsend Evans, and the late Catherine Marshall and her husband, Leonard LeSourd, were openly active in the movement. Mrs. LeSourd, widow of Senate chaplain Peter Marshall, had over 18 million of her books sold before her death in 1983. Those books recounting her charismatic experiences were *Something More* and *The Helper*.[14]

An important addition to the movement came in 1965 when J. Rodman Williams was baptized in the Holy Spirit while serving as professor of systematic theology at the Austin Presbyterian Theological Seminary in Texas. Already an able and well-known theologian among Presbyterians, Williams added serious theological depth to the charismatic movement as a whole. In later years he made great contributions through his books and teaching positions at Melodyland and the school of theology at CBN University. Especially influential was Williams' book, *The Pentecostal Reality*. Presbyterian theologian Charles Farah served the renewal in a similar fashion from his teaching position at Oral Roberts University.[15]

In 1974, the Charismatic Communion of Presbyterian Ministers changed its name to the Presbyterian Charismatic Communion. This change was brought about because of the thousands of laymen who wished to join the ministry of the group. Another change was effected in 1984 when the name was again changed, this time to Presbyterian and Reformed Renewal Ministries, International.[16]

By 1985, the PRRM counted almost 1,000 clergy members of the 2,500 to 3,000 who had been baptized in the Holy Spirit. The total membership of the group is about 5,000 contributing members. This relatively small group is representative of some 250,000 charismatics in the Presbyterian and Reformed churches in the United States. The PRRM organization publishes a bi-monthly magazine titled *Renewal News* which serves as a clearinghouse for conferences and developments among Presbyterian charismatics.[17]

Some of the Presbyterian churches that have been renewed in the Holy Spirit are the following: New Covenant Presbyterian, Pompano Beach, Florida, George Callahan, pastor; St. Giles Presbyterian, Richmond,

Virginia, Louis Skidmore, pastor; St. Giles, Charlotte, North Carolina, Percy Burns, pastor; Hope Presbyterian, Portland, Oregon, Larry Trogen, pastor; Bethany Presbyterian, Seattle, Washington, Dick Denham, pastor; Silverlake Presbyterian, Los Angeles, California, Bob Whitaker, pastor; Trinity Presbyterian, San Diego, California, Dick Adams, pastor; Our Lord's Community Church (RCA), Oklahoma City, Robert Wise, pastor; and Heights Cumberland Presbyterian Church in Albuquerque, New Mexico, Larry Moss, pastor.[18]

In addition to these congregations in the United States, charismatic Presbyterian churches flourish on the mission fields around the world. Especially powerful renewals are taking place in Brazil, Korea, New Zealand, Nigeria, Kenya, Uganda, Guatemala, Nicaragua and Taiwan.

Just as Presbyterians have been in the forefront of renewal in the past, one must assume that they will continue to provide leadership for the renewal of the churches in the future. The record shows that the Presbyterians have truly been pioneers in renewal, a fact that should be appreciated by all Christians of all churches.

For further information concerning the Presbyterian renewal, contact:
Brick Bradford, General Secretary
Presbyterian and Reformed Renewal Ministries
2245 N.W. 39th Street
Oklahoma City, OK 73112-8886
(405) 525-2552

The United Church of Christ Renewal

The United Church of Christ is one of the oldest denominations in the United States, a church that can trace its heritage to the Pilgrim fathers who landed at Plymouth Rock in 1620. These were the Puritans who fled to America to escape persecution from the established state church of England. Their struggle for religious liberty is part of the priceless heritage of American freedom.[1]

For over two centuries the Puritan church was known as the Congregational Church and was famous for its firm Calvinist theology, its local church autonomy and its strict Puritan life-style. In time, the Congregationalists spread from New England to all parts of the United States. The present United Church of Christ represents the merger of four different denominations over the years. The Congregational Christian Church, with roots in nineteenth-century Virginia, merged with the Congregationalists in 1931 to form the Congregational Christian Churches.[2]

In 1957 this church merged with the Evangelical and

Reformed Church which itself was the merger of two German-American churches with entirely different roots from the Congregationalists. These two churches, the German Reformed Church and the German Evangelical Synod of North America, merged in 1934 to form the Evangelical and Reformed Church in the U.S.

The denomination that resulted from these mergers in 1957 took the name United Church of Christ. This merger was unique in that the Evangelical and Reformed Church had its roots in German Calvinist piety while the Congregational Church came from distinctly English roots. Their governmental forms were also different. The Evangelical and Reformed Church had a more highly centralized government in contrast to the congregational polity seen in the very name of the Congregational Church.[3]

The UCC (as it is often called) is famous also for its theology which has caused it to be referred to as the most liberal denomination in the country. This openness to liberal ideas has ancient roots in the church, going back to the founding of the Unitarian movement in New England. Unitarians, who denied the Trinity, came mostly from Congregational backgrounds. The Unitarian Church was formed in 1825. Famous liberal leaders who remained in the church in the nineteenth century included Horace Bushnell, Henry Ward Beecher and George Washington Gladden, a father of the social gospel movement.[4]

In more recent times, the United Church of Christ has been a leader in many liberal social action causes that would have been inconceivable to the Pilgrim fathers. This has led to a general decline in the church, with heavy membership losses in recent years. Despite these tendencies, there have always been groups of evangelicals in the church who worked and prayed for a return to the solid evangelical faith of the Pilgrim fathers and the German reformers.

Renewal Movements in the UCC

In the past decade there have been increasing signs of spiritual renewal in the United Church of Christ which points to better things ahead. Four renewal movements in the church are strongly evangelical and are growing in numbers and influence. The first is the Biblical Witness Fellowship which began in 1977 as a group of evangelical pastors attempting to bring the church back to its biblical foundations. The second group is the spiritual development network made up of several renewal groups that are coordinated through the office of church life and leadership. This is the primary effort of the church hierarchy to bring about spiritual renewal in the denomination.[5]

Another effort at spiritual renewal within the UCC is an informal fellowship of theologians and pastors originally called the Biblical, Liturgical and Theological Study Group that eventually became known as the Craigville Colloquy. This is an annual workshop meeting for the purpose of drafting collective theological statements concerning the life of the church.[6]

Charismatic Renewal

The fourth group is the Fellowship of Charismatic Christians in the United Church of Christ. This group began in the late 1970s under the leadership of J. Ray Thompson, pastor of a UCC congregation in Reno, Nevada. Thompson was baptized in the Holy Spirit in 1972 and spoke in other tongues. After his Pentecostal experience, he hungered to find other charismatics in the church with whom he could share fellowship. The opportunity came in 1977 when the Kansas City Charismatic Conference brought together over 50,000 Christians from practically all denominations.[7]

At the suggestion of Reuben Sheares II, a denominational leader, Thompson ran a notice in a church periodical asking for charismatic members of the church to identify themselves. When about forty persons responded, Thompson sent out a series of newsletters suggesting that those interested meet in Kansas City to organize a charismatic group within the church. As a result of these efforts, seventy-three persons gathered in Kansas City on July 22, 1977, to form the Charismatic Fellowship in the United Church of Christ. A temporary steering committee of twelve persons was selected to serve with Thompson, who was elected chairman.[8]

The purpose of this new organization was to minister to the lonely and isolated charismatics in the church, establish a Christ-centered voice within the church and solidify the witness of the movement of the Holy Spirit in the United Church of Christ. The small but determined group left Kansas City with a vision to bring renewal to the church through the power and gifts of the Holy Spirit.

In 1978, representatives of the CCRCC met with Avery Post, president of the UCC, to discuss the goals and purposes of the fellowship. From that time forward, the charismatics have been a recognized force for renewal in the UCC. The liberal nature of the church made it easy for the charismatics to find acceptance, since the church showed the same openness to many other causes, some of which were extremely liberal.[9]

In August 1978, a new official name was chosen—

the Fellowship of Charismatic Christians in the United Church of Christ. In that year, the charismatics also joined forces with the Biblical Witness group in bringing a more biblical and evangelical emphasis to the denomination.[10]

Vernon Stoop and the FCC/UCC

Since 1979, when the FCC/UCC was restructured, the group has been led by several persons, including David Emmons, Robert Welsh and Robert Weeden. The present head of the FCC/UCC is Marion Fitkin of Toledo, Ohio. The director of services is Vernon Stoop, pastor of the Shepherd of the Hills UCC in Bechtelsville, Pennsylvania. Stoop also edits the *Focus Newsletter*, a periodical which serves as a clearinghouse of information for the movement. In addition to these responsibilities, Stoop serves as secretary of the Charismatic Concerns Committee and the North American Renewal Service Committee which planned the 1986 and 1987 New Orleans Congresses on the Holy Spirit and World Evangelization.[11]

The FCC/UCC is an active organization which sponsors several renewal programs for the church. These include the Acts Alive renewal conferences in which teams come to local churches for weekend events stressing lay witness, baptism in the Holy Spirit and the use of spiritual gifts. A second program called Ecclesia brings renewal services to local churches stressing body life. A third ministry is the King's Kids Camps, which brings hundreds of young people to the Lord each summer.

Several local parishes have experienced charismatic renewal in recent years. Among these are Trinity UCC in Mount Penn, Pennsylvania, James Miller, pastor;

Shepherd of the Hills UCC, Bechtelsville, Pennsylvania, Vernon Stoop, pastor; St. John's UCC, Massilon, Ohio, Robert Carleson, pastor; and Leidey's UCC, Sodderton, Pennsylvania, John Niederhaus, pastor.[12]

The Future

Charismatic leaders believe that a key to the future is the planting of new congregations which are charismatic from the beginning. In recent years young Spirit-filled pastors have pioneered dynamic new congregations that will serve as models for the future. The most notable of these is the Cornerstone Fellowship United Church of Christ in Post Falls, Idaho, which was formed in 1981 under the leadership of young pastor Loren Sandford. This is the only totally charismatic congregation in the denomination. The story of the founding of this church was told in the book *Birthing the Church* by Sandford.[13]

Another approach is the fostering of charismatic renewal in older congregations in a way that will promote unity and avoid divisiveness. Stoop's Shepherd of the Hills Church in Bechtelsville, Pennsylvania, is a model of this approach. This congregation, which is 150 years old, has been led by senior pastor Stoop for fifteen years. His goal has been to "bring about a marriage of a traditional non-charismatic congregation and those charismatic elements that have grown up within the fellowship without splitting the congregation." So far, this approach has proved successful at Shepherd of the Hills.[14]

Further information on the FCC/UCC may be obtained by writing to:

The United Church of Christ Renewal

Vernon Stoop
FCC/UCC
P.O. Box 12
Sassamansville, PA 19472

CHAPTER SIXTEEN

The Wesleyan Charismatics

For decades the words Wesleyan and charismatic have been seen as mutually exclusive terms. No group of churches has been more negative toward the gifts of the Spirit, especially that of tongues, than historic Holiness groups such as the Church of the Nazarene, the Wesleyan Church and the Church of God (Anderson, Indiana). At best, tongues have been looked on with suspicion, and at worst they have been dismissed.

This situation is remarkable in light of the historic fact that the Pentecostal movement originated in America and, indeed, around the world largely among Wesleyan-Holiness people. In fact, the original Pentecostals held to a basic belief in sanctification as a second work of grace and counted themselves as part of the Holiness movement. They simply added a third blessing called the baptism in the Holy Spirit evidenced by speaking with other tongues.[1]

With the organization of the Assemblies of God in 1914, many Pentecostals drifted from the Wesleyan camp, but about one half of American Pentecostals today still hold to a fundamentally Wesleyan-Arminian theology. It is generally agreed that classical Pentecostals share a common ancestry with the Holiness people and that the two movements are far more similar than they are different from each other.[2]

The Pentecostal Church of the Nazarene

The common roots of the two elements can be seen in the fact that the original name of the Church of the Nazarene was the Pentecostal Church of the Nazarene. However, the word Pentecostal was dropped from the name in 1919 to avoid confusion with the tongues-speakers who had pre-empted the name. The Nazarene position on tongues came when the founder of the church, Phineas Bresee, rejected the Azusa Street manifestations as invalid. His view was that the movement had as much effect in Los Angeles as a "pebble thrown into the sea."[3]

Bresee and his colleague, J.P. Widney, were quite willing to accept differences among early Nazarenes in matters they considered nonessential to salvation. Their early theme was "in essentials, unity; in non-essentials, liberty; in all things, charity." After Bresee's death, tongues were seen as a threat to the church, since so many Holiness people departed from their churches to form the first new Pentecostal denominations. The hardline anti-Pentecostal attitude of many Holiness people was summarized in Alma White's 1912 book entitled *Demons and Tongues*, which attributed all glossolalia to demonic influence.[4]

Other Holiness-type churches that rejected Pentecostalism included the Wesleyan Methodist Church, the Salvation Army, the Free Methodist Church, the Church of God (Anderson, Indiana) and the Pilgrim Holiness

Church. Holiness churches that accepted the Pentecostal message included the Church of God (Cleveland, Tennessee), the Pentecostal Holiness Church, the Church of God in Christ, the United Holy Church and the Pentecostal Freewill Baptist Church. These became the first organized Pentecostal denominations in America.[5]

John L. Peters and Warren Black

When the neo-Pentecostal movement began after 1960, it was inevitable that some Wesleyan-Holiness people would become involved again in the manifestations of the Holy Spirit. An early neo-Pentecostal was John L. Peters, formerly general secretary of the Nazarene Young People's Society and well-known historian of the Holiness movement. Although Peters had left the Nazarene church in 1948 to become a Methodist, his influence remained among many of his friends in the church. In 1962 Peters received the baptism in the Holy Spirit and spoke in tongues.[6]

In 1963, after hearing the testimony of Peters on one of John Osteen's broadcasts, Warren Black, controller of the Nazarene Publishing House in Kansas City, received the baptism in the Holy Spirit. After several days of prayer and fasting in his home, Black drew a circle on the floor, stepped inside the circle and promised God that he would seek Him until he was satisfied. "I was seeking God, not tongues," he said. What he received, however, was a powerful Pentecostal experience accompanied by speaking in tongues. At the same time he was instantly healed of a long-standing speech problem.[7]

Although divine healing was taught by the Nazarenes, tongues were still widely considered to be either fleshly or demonic. In 1971, as a result of his testimony before a Nazarene College student body, Black was put out of the church. Believing that his excommunication was done illegally, Black and other like-minded Nazarenes decided to take the charismatic question to the delegates of the highest body in the church, the General Assembly. Before this body met in Miami in 1972, all the delegates were sent a packet by mail explaining his position. Black was backed in this action by about twenty-five Nazarene members.[8]

Also presented to this assembly were four "memorials" from Nazarene districts calling on the church to disallow tongues in the churches. The appeals from Black "caused a furor" in the assembly. Many wanted to end the matter then and there by forbidding tongues forever. Others, led by Jack Ford of England, called for a study commission which could deal with the subject more dispassionately. Ford reminded the General Assembly that the Calvary Holiness denomination in England that merged with the Church of the Nazarene in 1955 had allowed tongues in the churches although the practice was not encouraged.[9]

Nazarenes Take a Stand

The General Assembly took no action in 1972, but to the surprise of Black and others, it was learned that the general superintendents had acted the previous year on their own when they issued their own interpretation of the *Manual*. Their statement, which lacked the authority of General Assembly action, stated that "speaking in tongues either as the evidence of the baptism with the Holy Spirit or as an ecstatic neo-Pentecostal prayer language is interpreted as inveighing against the doctrine and practices of the church."[10]

For thirteen years, the church operated under the

contradictions engendered by the Calvary Holiness precedent in England and the interpretation of the general superintendents. On the basis of the English precedent, Dan Brady, a pastor from Dayton, Ohio, who had been defrocked for speaking in tongues, appealed to be reinstated in the church. In 1985, his appeal was denied on the highest judicial level.[11]

This led the church to add an official statement on tongues in the *Manual* for the first time in history in the General Assembly which met in Anaheim, California, in 1985. The statement was placed in the appendix and now stands as the official policy of the church. After affirming that the biblical evidence of the baptism in the Holy Spirit is the "cleansing of the heart from sin" and the fruit of the Spirit, the article states: "To affirm that even a special or any alleged physical evidence or 'prayer language' is evidence of the baptism with the Holy Spirit is contrary to the biblical and historical position of the church."[12]

This statement, which does not actually forbid tongues, is a disavowal of the initial evidence theory propounded by the Pentecostals in the early part of the century. Very few charismatics in the mainline churches would disagree with this position as it relates to glossolalia. In effect, the working position of the church now seems to be that tongues would be allowed in private devotions as long as the practice is not propagated in such a way as to support the initial evidence theory or bring division to the churches. This would include the understanding that tongues would not be manifested in the public worship services of the church.

To many Nazarenes, however, the effect of this statement has been to outlaw tongues in the church. A case in point is the experience of Steve Gustin, pastor of a Nazarene congregation in Azusa, California. By 1986 this church was ninety percent charismatic and made attempts to stay in the denomination. But after the General Assembly passed the resolution on tongues in 1985, the Azusa congregation was expelled from the denomination. After leaving, the congregation took the name, Berean Christian Center. Whether other pastors or churches leave over the issue seems to depend on how church authorities interpret the language of the 1985 statement.[13]

Other Holiness Churches Speak Out

A position similar to that of the Nazarenes was taken in June 1986 by the general assembly of the Church of God (Anderson, Indiana). For many years local churches of this denomination have added the word "non-Pentecostal" in their advertising to distinguish them from the many Pentecostal groups that use variations of the name Church of God. After a year-long study, the assembly adopted a special study commission report which in general restated the church's historic position that tongues are not the initial evidence of the baptism in the Holy Spirit.

The report did, however, allow that tongues is one of the authentic gifts of the Spirit for today and did not disallow their use in private devotions. Like the Nazarenes, the Church of God seems willing to accommodate glossolalics who do not publicly display, or promote divisively, the gift of tongues.[14]

In spite of the rigid historical position of these and other Holiness churches many pastors and laymen have spoken in tongues over the years. Pastors in such situations have usually been removed from their pulpits immediately when authorities heard of their experiences. Among Nazarenes who have been excommunicated over the years are Wilbur Jackson, Merrill Bolender, Wayne Buchart, Jerry Love, Robert Mueller, Stan Pulliam, Jep Anderson and David Alsobrook. Ray Bringham, a well-known charismatic leader from the Church of God, has led a struggle for many years to bring renewal back to his church.[15]

Wilbur Jackson and the WCF

In recent years, many of these former pastors have met together in conferences sponsored by Wilbur Jackson's King's Mountain Faith Fellowship in Cincinnati, Ohio. Jackson, pastor of the Lockland Nazarene Church in Cincinnati, was separated from the Church of the Nazarene in 1971 after his Pentecostal experience became known. He has become the acknowledged leader of the group that would still like to see a charismatic renewal in the church.[16]

In 1979, in a meeting of like-minded ministers, he formed the Wesleyan-Holiness Charismatic Fellowship for ministry to those who had suffered rejection by the churches. In 1977, a group of these men met in Kansas City to plan strategies for the future. In 1985, the organization was reorganized and strengthened. This group also planned a session to meet in the New Orleans Congresses on the Holy Spirit and World Evangelization in 1986 and 1987.[17]

A sign of rapprochement for the future was the recent publication of Howard Snyder's book, *The Divided Flame: Wesleyans and the Charismatic Renewal* (1986). This volume is a plea for those in the Wesleyan tradition to open their churches to the gifts of the Holy Spirit. Snyder contends that Wesley himself was charismatic and that, indeed, all churches are by definition charismatic or they are not fully Christian. He contends also that Holiness churches should enter into dialogue with charismatic Christianity since each side could learn from the other.[18]

Since the Nazarene statement of 1985 and the Church of God statement of 1986 did not forbid tongues, but only the teaching that tongues constitute the initial evidence of the baptism in the Holy Spirit, the door may be open for Nazarenes and other Wesleyans to pray in tongues and remain in the churches.

For further information on the Wesleyan-Holiness Charismatic Fellowship, contact:
Wilbur Jackson
Wesleyan-Holiness Charismatic Fellowship
P.O. Box 24008
Cincinnati, OH 45224
(513) 761-3372

CHAPTER SEVENTEEN

Conclusions

Any movement of significance is eventually shaped by leaders that pioneer its beginning and later ones that emerge to define and direct its ongoing development. It has been said that Pentecostalism is a "movement without a man," that is, without an outstanding founder such as a Luther, a Calvin or a Wesley. Instead, the movements I have described in the foregoing chapters were led by many men and women of staunch faith and fearless courage who laid down their lives for a cause that to them was dearer than wealth or the plaudits of men.

For the classical Pentecostals, the movement was a "vision of the disinherited" in the words of John Mapes Anderson. Starting among the poor and outcast of society, they offered new hope to millions of deprived and marginal people often ignored by the mainline "respectable" churches. The new struggling churches formed by the Pentecostal movement represented a "haven for the masses," as described by Epinay. The founders of the Pentecostal denominations made heroic sacrifices in building these churches. In doing so they often endured the persecution and misunderstanding that is the usual lot of the religious revolutionary. As a result of their faithfulness, the names of Charles Parham, William Seymour, Charles H. Mason, Joseph H. King, Ambrose J. Tomlinson, Eudorus N. Bell and Aimee Semple McPherson will take their places on the pages of church history.

The names of the founders and leaders of the charismatic renewal movements in the mainline churches are less well-known to many church historians. This is due, of course, to the relative newness of these movements in comparison to the earlier ones. As time goes on, such names as Richard Winkler, Gerald Derstine, Harald Bredesen, James Brown, Dennis Bennett, Larry Christenson, Charles Simpson, Kevin Ranaghan, Ralph Martin and Nelson Litwiller will take their places with other more familiar names of church history.

Several leaders of the charismatic renewal have established themselves as theological standard-bearers for the movement as a whole. Their work has been quite influential in the development of a charismatic theology. In this area the name of Kilian McDonnell stands out above the rest. His early theological formulations and continuing historical and sociological studies have established him as the most influential theological and intellectual leader of the movement in the liturgical churches. Other Catholic writers such as Edward O'Connor, Francis Martin and Cardinal Suenens have also vastly influenced the Catholic charismatic renewal movement.

Similar contributions among mainline Protestants have been made by Howard Ervin, Larry Christenson and

J. Rodman Williams. Among classical Pentecostals the names of Donald Gee and David du Plessis stand out as ecumenical thinkers and activists. Other classical Pentecostals who have made important theological contributions over the years include Joseph King, William Durham and Harold Horton.

In the past decade, a small group of charismatic leaders with translocal ministries has also exercised a continuing influence on the direction of the movement in general. These are the men who have attended the gatherings in Glencoe, Missouri, known as the Charismatic Concerns Committee. This has been a low key, low profile meeting that has exercised a leavening influence on the movements involved. Led for a decade by Larry Christenson and Kevin Ranaghan, this gathering of about fifty persons has aided in resolving several differences that have arisen between leaders of the various groups as well as serving as a spiritual think-tank for the movement at large.

Along with Christenson and Ranaghan, some of the influential participants at Glencoe over the years have been Charles Simpson, Bob Mumford, Derek Prince, Brick Bradford, Nelson Litwiller, Ross Whetstone, Carleton Spencer, Joseph Garlington, Vinson Synan, Karl Strader and Vernon Stoop. In 1984, Synan and Stoop were chosen to lead the Glencoe meetings.

Kansas City Charismatic Conference

Out of these gatherings came the inspiration and leadership for the Kansas City Charismatic Conference that met in Kansas City in 1977. The chairman of that conference was Kevin Ranaghan who was assisted by a fourteen-man planning committee consisting of the leaders of the constituent groups that sponsored the conference. Members of the committee were Brick Bradford, Larry Christenson, Ithiel Clemmons, Howard Courtney, Robert Frost, Roy Lamberth, Nelson Litwiller, Bob Mumford, Ken Pagard, Kevin Ranaghan, Carleton Spencer, David Stern and Ross Whetstone. Using the "three streams" approach, Ranaghan (Roman Catholic), Christenson (Protestant) and Synan (Pentecostal) served as an executive committee to pastor the conference.

About 52,000 persons registered for the Kansas City conference, which many regard as the high-water mark of the charismatic renewal up to that time. In David Barrett's *World Christian Encyclopedia*, this conference was listed as one of the noteworthy events in the 2,000-year history of Christianity.

Kansas City marked the first time that all the various segments of the Pentecostal/charismatic renewal met together at the same time and place. It was probably the largest ecumenical conference ever convened in the history of the nation. The unique dynamic of the gathering was the fact that Christians of practically all denominations met together in a demonstration of grassroots unity never seen before in America.

The Kansas City conference was unique in that fourteen separate subconferences convened in morning denominational sessions, while common workshops were offered to all participants in the afternoons. At night all differences were laid aside as the participants worshipped side by side in Arrowhead Stadium. The conference theme, "Jesus Is Lord," not only became the standard uniting the worshippers into one body, but also became a universal slogan for the movement in the following decade.

Conclusions

In the years that followed 1977, the Glencoe leaders considered the possibility of conducting another such conference, a "Kansas City II," as it was called. However, year after year the leaders felt that the time was not yet ripe for another such meeting. But in 1985 there came a unanimous conviction that the Lord's time had come to plan for another one.

The Future

The vision that unfolded in Glencoe was to hold a leaders' congress in 1986 in a large city intended for 5,000 to 10,000 pastors and prayer group leaders. This would be followed in 1987 by a general congress similar to the one in Kansas City. It was also conjectured that as many as 75,000 participants might register for it. At the same time other continental congresses would be planned to convene in Africa, Europe, the Far East and Latin America.

A group of international leaders was given a further vision for a world congress to be held in a world-class city in 1990 or 1991. This congress would inaugurate a decade of world evangelization which would last until the end of the century. Those who first shared in this vision were Larry Christenson, Kevin Ranaghan, Tom Forrest, Michael Harper and Bill Burnett. Later, at the suggestion of John Wimber, it was decided that all these gatherings would be called Congresses on the Holy Spirit and World Evangelization, emphasizing the use of signs and wonders in converting the world to Jesus Christ.

Tom Forrest, a Redemptorist priest, also received an electrifying vision for the end of the century which the planners of the congresses enthusiastically adopted. Forrest's vision was to call on the churches of the world to join in a massive evangelistic effort to bring millions of people to the Lord before the end of the century. The goal would be for the church to offer to Jesus, on the celebration of His birthday, December 25, 2000 A.D., an absolute majority of the human race as Christians. In 1985, only one-third of the world population claimed to be Christian in any sense of the word. To present Jesus with over half the world population as Christian would mean that every congregation and denomination would have to double its membership in only fifteen years.

This vision dominated the atmosphere of the 1985 leaders' congress which convened in the New Orleans Superdome in October 1986. There over 7,500 leaders gathered to hear such leaders as Oral Roberts, Paul Yonggi Cho, John Wimber, Terry Fullam and Tom Forrest unfold this vision of world evangelization. Chairman Vinson Synan challenged participants to become the "shock troops" that would take the struggle into the territory of the enemy in the last great spiritual crusade of the millenium. Terry Fullam challenged the conference to take the battle even further—behind enemy lines—to win the world for Christ.

As the year 2000 A.D. approaches, many strident voices will prophesy the end of the world. Many weird sects and cults will arise exploiting the apocalyptic atmosphere of the times. In the midst of this, one could pray that the loudest and most productive voices of all will be those of a vast army of evangelists who will go to the ends of the earth with the good news that Jesus Christ is Lord to the glory of God the Father.

This great and noble vision should well consume the energy and resources of the Christian communities for the rest of the century. But, sad to say, it will not take place at the present growth of the churches. According to Barrett, the percentage of Christians in the world population has actually been falling since the turn of the century.

In order for the churches to reach the goal of a world Christian majority by 2000 A.D., one of the greatest revivals the world has ever seen would have to take place in the next dozen years. The church will never accomplish this goal using the traditional methods of the past. Perhaps the secret will be for Christians in Third World nations that are experiencing mighty revivals to become evangelists to the Western nations. Perhaps the great spiritual revolutions that are now taking place in Korea, China and Latin America will spill over into Europe and North America.

Other forces are also girding for battle to win the world by the year 2000 A.D. The communists now control over one-third of the world's population and their revolutionary fervor has not waned with the passing of the decades. The Moslems and Mormons have both targeted London and Paris for conversion. They are sending thousands of missionaries and untold millions of dollars into their proselyting efforts. Meanwhile, Pope John Paul II has spoken of the possibility that Russian Christians may be the ones that will re-Christianize Europe.

Perhaps from the Congresses on the Holy Spirit and World Evangelization, the Lord will raise up an army of apostles, prophets, pastors, teachers and evangelists who will fan out over the world "with signs following" to win the world for Christ before the end of the century.

THE 20TH-CENTURY PENTECOSTAL EXPLOSION

In the Superdome in New Orleans, on October 8, 1986, a trumpet sounded calling the leaders together. This was done in accordance to the Old Testament practice of calling the elders together by the signal of one silver trumpet sounding a fanfare (Numbers 10). At the end of the leaders' congress, two trumpets sounded calling the people to a general congress in 1987. The trumpet will also sound in 1990 calling Christians to a world congress in a great world-class city.

Perhaps the church is a sleeping giant which will arouse itself and go forth into battle equipped with the gifts of the Holy Spirit. If so, the last years of the second millennium may well be the best in the history of the church.

Blow the trumpet in Zion,
Sanctify a fast, call a solemn assembly:
Gather the people, sanctify the congregation,
Assemble the elders, gather the children,
And those that nurse the breasts:
Let the bridegroom go forth out of his chamber,
And the bride come out of her closet.
Let the priests, the ministers of the Lord,
Weep between the porch and the altar...

And it shall come to pass afterward,
That I will pour out my Spirit upon all flesh,
And your sons and your daughters shall prophesy,
Your old men shall dream dreams,
Your young men shall see visions:
And also upon the servants and upon the handmaids
In those days I will pour out my Spirit...

Conclusions

And it shall come to pass,
That whosoever shall call on the name of the Lord
Shall be delivered...."
Joel 2:15-17;28-29;32

Notes

CHAPTER 1
The Assemblies of God

1. Major histories of the Assemblies of God include: Carl Brumback, *Suddenly... From Heaven: A History of the Assemblies of God* (Springfield, Mo., 1961) 380 p.; Klaud Kendrick, *The Promise Fulfilled: A History of the Modern Pentecostal Movement* (Springfield, Mo., 1961), 273 p.; William Menzies, *Anointed to Serve: The Story of the Assemblies of God* (Springfield, Mo., 1971), 436 p.; and Edith Waldvogel Blumhofer, *The Assemblies of God: A Popular History* (Springfield, Mo., 1985), 160 p.
Also useful for the Assemblies of God and other classical Pentecostal groups are Robert Mapes Anderson, *Vision of the Disinherited: The Making of American Pentecostalism* (New York, 1979), 326 p.; and Vinson Synan, *The Holiness-Pentecostal Movement in the United States* (Grand Rapids, 1971), 239 p.

2. Menzies, *Anointed to Serve*, 64-76; 48-49; 70-71; Anderson, *Vision of the Disinherited*, 188-194; Synan, *Holiness-Pentecostal Movement*, 133-137, 141-153. Also see William Menzies, "Non-Wesleyan Origins of the Pentecostal Movement," in Vinson Synan, *Aspects of Pentecostal Charismatic Origins* (Plainfield, N.J., 1975), 81-98.

3. Anderson, *Vision of the Disinherited*, 188-194; Synan, *Holiness-Pentecostal Movement*, 165-171.

4. Anderson, *Vision of the Disinherited*, 173-184; Richard A. Lewis, "E.N. Bell: An Early Pentecostal Spokesman" (Paper presented to the Society for Pentecostal Studies, November 14, 1986, in Costa Mesa, Calif.), 15 p.

5. Brumback, *Suddenly...From Heaven*, 88-97; John S. Sawin, "The Response and Attitude of Dr. A. B. Simpson and the Christian and Missionary Alliance to the Tongues Movement of 1906-1920" (Paper presented to the Society for Pentecostal Studies, November 14, 1986, in Costa Mesa, Calif.), 72 p.

6. Synan, *Holiness-Pentecostal Movement*, 150; Brumback, *Suddenly...From Heaven*, 99-103.

199

THE 20TH-CENTURY PENTECOSTAL EXPLOSION

7. J. Roswell Flower, "History of the Assemblies of God" (n.p., n.d.), 17-19; Menzies, *Anointed to Serve*, 92-105.

8. Menzies, *Anointed to Serve*, 80-105; Brumback, *Suddenly...From Heaven*, 151-171.

9. These reasons were listed in the "call" in *Word and Witness*, December 10, 1913, 1; see Brumback, *Suddenly...From Heaven*, 157, for a photocopy of the call.

10. Ibid., 168-169.

11. Ibid., 216-225; Menzies, *Anointed to Serve*, 129, 320.

12. Menzies, *Anointed to Serve*, 106-121. Also see Brumback's answer to the oneness movement in *God in Three Persons* (Cleveland, Tenn., 1959).

13. Synan, *Holiness-Pentecostal Movement*, 157-158; Menzies, *Anointed to Serve*, 384-390.

14. For the Assemblies of God statement on the charismatic renewal movement, see Kilian McDonnell, *Presence, Power, Praise: Documents on the Charismatic Renewal*, 3 vols. (Collegeville, Minn., 1980); Vol. I, 318. Also see Blumhofer, *The Assemblies of God*, 113-117, 141.

15. Jae Bum Lee, "Pentecostal Distinctives and Protestant Church Growth in Korea." Ph.D. dissertation, Fuller Theological Seminary, 1986, 313 p.; 169-228.

16. See *Assemblies of God: Who We Are and What We Believe* (Springfield, Mo., 1984), 23 p.; *A/G Facts, Current Information About the Assemblies of God* (Springfield, Mo.: Office of Information, 1984).

CHAPTER 2
The Baptist Renewal

1. John Osteen, personal interview with the author, Tulsa, Okla., June 24, 1986.

2. See R.G. Torbet, *A History of the Baptists*, rev. ed. (Philadelphia, 1963), 17-168.

3. Ibid., 62-83; also see A.C. Underwood, *A History of the English Baptists* (London, 1947), 286 p.

4. Torbet, *A History of the Baptists*, 201-512.

5. See W.L. Lumpkin, *Baptist Confessions of Faith* (Chicago, 1959), 430 p.; and I.J. Van Ness, *The Baptist Spirit* (Nashville, 1914), 327 p.

6. Edward T. Hiscox, *The New Directory for Baptist Churches* (Philadelphia, 1894), 354-363, 536-537.

7. Charles H. Spurgeon, "On the Holy Spirit," *Spurgeon's Sermons* (Grand Rapids, Mich., reprint from 1857), I, 129-130; A.J. Gordon, *The Ministry of Healing, Miracles of Cure in All Ages* (Harrisburg, Pa., 1961), 224 p.; J. Gilchrist Lawson, *Deeper Experiences of Famous Christians* (Anderson, Ind., 1911), 329-336.

8. Synan, *Holiness-Pentecostal Movement*, 124, 130-131.

9. Ibid.

10. "But What About Hicks?" *Christian Century*, July 7, 1954, 814-815; Synan, *In the Latter Days*, 25.

11. Jamie Buckingham, personal interview with the author, Tulsa, Okla., June 24, 1986.

12. David Manuel, *Like a Mighty River: A Personal Account of the Conference of 1977* (Orleans, Mass., 1977), 117.

200

Notes

13. Howard Ervin, personal interview with the author, Green Lake, Wis., July 8, 1986. Howard Ervin, *These Are Not Drunken As Ye Suppose* (Plainfield, N.J., 1967).

14. Gary Clark and Charles Moore, personal interviews with the author, Green Lake, Wis., July 9, 1986; Gary Clark, "An Extra Dimension," *Christian Life*, August 1985, 36-39.

15. Pat Robertson, *Shout It From the Housetops* (Plainfield, N.J., 1972), 255 p.; Harald Bredesen, *Yes, Lord* (Plainfield, N.J., 1972), 172-180.

16. Ray and Marjorie Bess, personal interview with the author, Green Lake, Wis., July 9, 1986. Also a personal letter from Marjorie Bess dated July 26, 1986.

17. Gary Clark, Synan interview.

18. See Synan, *In the Latter Days*, (Ann Arbor, Mich., 1984), 136-139.

19. Clark Whitten, personal interview with the author, Oklahoma City, Okla., August 18, 1986; Clark Whitten, "Profile in Grace," *Fulness Magazine*, July-August 1986, 9-11.

20. Ibid.

21. Larry Lea, personal interview with the author, Tulsa, Okla., June 6, 1986.

22. W. Leroy Martin, personal interview with the author, Tulsa, Okla., June 7, 1986.

23. Don Le Master, personal interview with the author, Fort Lauderdale, Fla., August 23, 1986.

24. James Robison, "Restoration Report," *Days of Restoration*, May-June 1986, 11-13.

25. Ras Robinson, "Who are You Who Read *Fulness*?" *Fulness Magazine*, July-August 1986, 4.

26. Le Master, Synan interview.

27. Kenneth Kantzer, "The Charismatics Among Us," *Christianity Today*, February 22, 1980, 25-29.

CHAPTER 3
The Catholic Charismatic Renewal

1. This account is based on personal interviews with Patti Gallagher Mansfield by the author in New Orleans, January 1986, as well as her "Come, Holy Spirit: A Testimony by Patti Mansfield" (Paper read at the 1986 National Leaders' Conference held at Steubenville, Ohio). Also see her "Come, Holy Spirit," in *New Covenant*, February 1986, 8-10. Other sources include Kevin and Dorothy Ranaghan, *Catholic Pentecostals* (New York, 1969), 6-37.

2. Ibid., 38-57, Bertil Ghezzi and Kevin Ranaghan, personal interviews with the author, 1985-1986; Edward D. O'Connor, *The Pentecostal Movement in the Catholic Church* (Notre Dame, Ind., 1971), 15-16.

3. Synan, *In the Latter Days*, 97-118; Ranaghan, *Catholic Pentecostals*, 48-50.

4. Ibid., 48-50.

5. Ibid., 44-46.

6. Richard Quebedeaux, *The New Charismatics II* (San Francisco, 1983), 78.

7. Florence Adeline Dodge, personal interview with the author, Pittsburgh, Pa., May 23, 1986.

8. Ibid.

THE 20TH-CENTURY PENTECOSTAL EXPLOSION

9. Edward D. O'Connor, "The Hidden Roots of the Charismatic Renewal in the Catholic Church," in Vinson Synan, *Aspects of Pentecostal/Charismatic Origins* (Plainfield, N.J., 1975), 169-192.

10. See Bert Ghezzi, "Three Charismatic Communities," in Kevin and Dorothy Ranaghan, eds. *As the Spirit Leads Us* (New York, 1971), 164-186; Steven B. Clark, *Building Christian Communities* (Notre Dame, Ind., 1971).

11. Quebedeaux, *The New Charismatics II*, 78-79. Also see Leon Joseph Cardinal Suenens, *A New Pentecost?* (New York, 1974); John C. Houghey, "The Holy Spirit: A Ghost No Longer," *America*, (June 16, 1973), 551; Mary Ann Jahr, "A Turning Point," *New Covenant* (August 1974), 4.

12. Quebedeaux, *The New Charismatics II*, 79; Manuel, *Like a Mighty River*, 156-176.

13. See Synan, *In the Latter Days*, 106-109.

14. McDonnell, *Presence, Power, Praise*, I, 207-210, 364-368, 580-584.

15. Early theological works include: Kilian McDonnell, *Catholic Pentecostalism: Problems in Evaluation* (Pecos, New Mexico, 1970); Donald Gelpi, *Pentecostalism: A Theological Viewpoint* (New York, 1971). Kevin and Dorothy Ranaghan's *Catholic Pentecostals* (1969) and O'Connor's *The Pentecostal Movement in the Catholic Church* (1971) also offered preliminary theological insights and evaluations.

16. McDonnell, *Presence, Power, Praise*, III, 70-75; *New Covenant*, July 1975, 23-25.

17. Joy Lepage Smith, "On Retreat," *New Covenant*, 1984, 14.

18. Bill Beatty, personal interview with the author, Chicago, Ill., November 4, 1986.

19. James Manney, "Father Michael Scanlan and the University of Steubenville," *New Covenant*, September 1985, 10-14.

20. David Barrett, *World Christian Encyclopedia* (New York, 1982), 820.

21. Fred Lilly, "Unity in Christ," *New Covenant*, December 1986, 12-13; Julia Duin, "Signs and Wonders in New Orleans," *Christianity Today*, November 21, 1986, 26-27; Steve Lawson, "Leaders Unite in New Orleans," *Charisma*, December 1986, 58-59.

CHAPTER 4
The Churches of Christ Renewal

1. Jamie Buckingham, "The Music of Spiritual Awakening: Belmont Church of Christ, Nashville, Tennessee," *Charisma*, July 1984, 32-37.

2. The best history of the restoration tradition is Winfred Ernest Garrison and Alfred DeGroot's *The Disciples of Christ: A History*, rev. ed. (St. Louis, 1958), 592 p. Also important are William Garrett West's *Barton Warren Stone: Early American Advocate of Christian Unity* (Nashville, 1954); and Leroy Garrett, *The Stone-Campbell Movement* (Joplin, Mo.: College Press Company, 1981), 739 p. The definitive social history is David Edwin Harrell Jr. *Quest for a Christian America: The Disciples and American Society*, 2 vols. (Nashville, 1966).

3. Barton Stone, *The Biography of Eld. Barton Stone, Written by Himself With Additions and Reflections* (Cincinnati, 1847), 34-43; Max Ward Randall, *The Great Awakening and the Restoration Movement* (Joplin, Mo., 1983), 48-71.

4. Garrison and DeGroot, *The Disciples of Christ*, 124-179.

202

Notes

5. Ibid., 212-217.

6. Ibid., 173, 183-187f.

7. Garrison and DeGroot, *The Disciples of Christ*, 402-446.

8. Ibid., 404; Garrett, *The Stone-Campbell Movement*, 573-614.

9. Ibid., 615-654.

10. Constance Jacquet, *Yearbook of American and Canadian Churches, 1984* (Nashville, 1984), 231-238.

11. Pat Boone, *A New Song* (Carol Stream, Ill., 1970), 5-46.

12. Buckingham, "Music of Spiritual Awakening," 36.

13. Ibid.

14. Ibid.

15. Jim Bevis, personal interview with the author, New Orleans, September 15, 1986.

16. Ibid.

17. Ibid.; Robert Yawberg, *Diary*, April 24-26, 1978.

18. Letters of invitation to friends from Bevis and Finto, December 6, 1979. Also see George Ambrose, "God Said It. I Believe It. That Settles It: Spiritual Renewal in the Church of Christ," *Charisma*, July 1984, 71-72.

19. Jim Bevis, Synan interview.

20. See Tom Smith, "Welcome to Conference '86," *Paraclete Journal*, July 1986, 2.

CHAPTER 5
The Churches of God

1. The standard history of the Church of God (Cleveland, Tennessee) is Charles W. Conn's *Like a Mighty Army: A History of the Church of God, 1886-1976*, rev. ed. (Cleveland, Tenn., 1977). The history of the Church of God of Prophecy is given in Charles Davidson's *Upon This Rock* (Cleveland, Tenn., 1973-1976). 3 vols. An extensive biography of A.J. Tomlinson is Lillie Duggar's *A.J. Tomlinson, Former General Overseer of the Church of God* (Cleveland, Tenn., 1964), 807 p.

2. Conn, *Like a Mighty Army*, 1-18; Synan, *Holiness-Pentecostal Movement*, 80-83; Davidson, *Upon This Rock, 1*, 284-300.

3. A.J. Tomlinson, *Answering the Call of God* (Cleveland, Tenn., 1942), 1-15.

4. See Homer Tomlinson, *The Shout of a King* (New York, 1965), 14-20; and Duggar, *A.J. Tomlinson*, 30-45.

5. Tomlinson, *Answering the Call*, 17.

6. L. Howard Juillerat, *Book of Minutes, General Assemblies, Churches of God* (Cleveland, Tenn., 1922), 15-19; Conn, *Like a Mighty Army*, 61-69.

7. Juillerat, *Book of Minutes*, 15-19.

8. See Homer A. Tomlinson, ed., *Diary of A.J. Tomlinson, 1901-1923* (New York, 1949), 68-72.

9. Synan, *Holiness-Pentecostal Movement*, 133-135.

10. Ibid.; Tomlinson, *Answering the Call of God*, 9-10.

11. Charles E. Jones, *A Guide to the Study of the Pentecostal Movement* (Metuchen, N.J., 1983), Vol. I, 271.

12. Conn, *Like a Mighty Army*, 175-190; Tomlinson, *Answering the Call*, 8;

THE 20TH-CENTURY PENTECOSTAL EXPLOSION

Davidson, *Upon This Rock, I*, 573-610.

13. Synan, *Holiness-Pentecostal Movement*, 194-195; Davidson, *Upon This Rock*, I, 610-648; Conn, *Like a Mighty Army*, 1-18.

14. Ibid., 195-197; Tomlinson, *The Shout of a King*, 1-219; John Nichols, *Pentecostalism* (New York, 1966), 139-143.

15. The record of Church of God (Cleveland, Tennessee) foreign missions is given in Charles W. Conn's *Where the Saints Have Trod* (Cleveland, Tenn., 1959), 312 p.

16. Lewis J. Willis, personal interview with the author, Oklahoma City, Okla., May 5, 1986.

17. Harold Hunter, personal interview with the author, Cleveland, Tenn., September 4, 1986.

CHAPTER 6
The Church of God in Christ

1. Jacquet, *Yearbook of American and Canadian Churches 1984*, 40-43; 232.

2. Charles Harrison Mason, *The History and Life of Elder C.H. Mason* (Memphis, 1920), 97 p. This book has been reprinted and revised several times since 1920, the latest version being J.O. Patterson, German R. Rose and Julia Mason Atkins, *History and Formative Years of the Church of God in Christ With Excerpts From the Life and Works of Its Founder— Bishop C.H. Mason* (Memphis, Tenn., 1969), 143 p.

3. Patterson, *History and Formative Years*, 14-17; Otho B. Cobbins, ed. *History of the Church of Christ (Holiness) U.S.A.* (New York, 1966), 1-27; David M. Tucker, *Black Pastors and Leaders: Memphis, 1819-1972* (Memphis, 1975), 87-88.

4. Kendrick, *The Promise Fulfilled*, 16. Also see Phillip Garvin, *Religious America* (New York, 1974), 141-169; Cobbins, *History of the Church of God (Holiness)*, 117-120; Patterson, *History and Formative Years*, 63-64.

5. James Tinney, "Black Pentecostals Convene," *Christianity Today*, December 4, 1970, 36. Also see Tinney, "Black Pentecostals: Setting Up the Kingdom," *Christianity Today*, December 5, 1975, 42-43; Patterson, *History and Formative Years*, 63.

6. Ibid., 17-20; Kendrick, *The Promise Fulfilled*, 16; Synan, *Holiness-Pentecostal Movement*, 165-184.

7. Leonard Lovett, "Black Origins of the Pentecostal Movement," in Synan, *Aspects of Pentecostal/Charismatic Origins*, 123-141; Tucker, *Black Pastors and Leaders*, 90-94; Patterson, *History and Formative Years*, 17-20.

8. Cobbins, *History of the Church of Christ (Holiness)* 16, 50-52. Also see Nils-Bloch Hoell, *The Pentecostal Movement, Its Origin, Development, and Distinctive Character* (Oslo, Norway, 1964), 56-64.

9. Patterson, *History and Formative Years*, 46-55, 66-69; J. Gordon Melton, *Biographical Dictionary of American Cult and Sect Leaders* (New York, 1986), 170-171; Arthur Piepkorn, *Profiles in Belief...Holiness and Pentecostal*, Vol. III (San Francisco, 1979), 110-112.

10. Tucker, *Black Pastors and Leaders*, 97-99. Ithiel Clemmons, personal interview with the author, Oklahoma City, Okla., January 29, 1986.

11. Ibid.; Synan, *Holiness-Pentecostal Movement*, 168-169.

Notes

12. Howard N. Kenyon, "Black Experience in the Assemblies of God" (Paper read at the Society for Pentecostal Studies, November 15, 1986, Costa Mesa, Calif.); Synan, *Holiness-Pentecostal Movement*, 178-179.

13. Ibid., 149-153. Also see Menzies, *Anointed to Serve*, 370.

14. Arnor S. Davis, "The Pentecostal Movement in Black Christianity," *Black Church*, 2:1 (1972), 65-88. Also see the U.S. Bureau of the Census reports for 1926 and 1936 under "Church of God in Christ. Statistics, denominational history, doctrine, and organization." (Washington, D.C.: U.S. Government Printing Office, 1929 and 1940).

15. Ithiel Clemmons, Synan interview; Patterson, *History and Formative Years*, 71-75.

16. Ibid., 77-92.

17. Piepkorn, *Profiles in Belief*, 18-19; Jacquet, *Yearbook 1984*, 18-19, 110-112.

CHAPTER 7
The Episcopal Renewal

1. See Dennis Bennett, *Nine O'Clock in the Morning* (Plainfield, N.J., 1970), 1-30.

2. Liston Pope, *Millhands and Preachers, A Study of Gastonia* (New Haven, 1946), 138.

3. Bennett, *Nine O'Clock*, 61.

4. See *Time* magazine, March 29, 1963, 52; August 15, 1963, 52-55.

5. Michael Harper, *As at the Beginning: The Twentieth-Century Pentecostal Revival* (Plainfield, N.J., 1965), 34-39. Also see Harper's *Three Sisters*, (Wheaton, Ill., 1979).

6. Richard Winkler, personal interview with the author, Maui, Hawaii, January 11, 1986.

7. See McDonnell, *Presence, Power, Praise*, I, 10-20. For the report coming out of the Bennett case, see Vol. I, 1-21.

8. Frank Farrell, "Outburst of Tongues: The New Penetration," *Christianity Today*, September 13, 1963, 3-7.

9. Synan, *In the Latter Days*, 89-95.

10. McDonnell, *Presence, Power, Praise*, I, 96-104.

11. Bennett, *Nine O'Clock*, 73-90; personal interview with the author, Kansas City, July 1977. Also see John Sherrill, *They Speak With Other Tongues* (New York, 1964), 61-66.

12. Quebedeaux, *The New Charismatics II*, 58, 140-141, 156, 179.

13. Ibid., 78-81, 102-104, 149-152. Also see Jean Stone and Harald Bredesen, *The Charismatic Renewal in the Historic Churches* (Van Nuys, Calif., 1963).

14. McDonnell, *Presence, Power, Praise*, I, 20.

15. For the Fountain Trust story, see Quebedeaux, *New Charismatics II*, 98-105.

16. Terry Fullam, personal interview with the author, August 6, 1986. See Steve Lawson, "Episcopal Renewal on the Move," *Charisma*, March 1986, 64.

17. Much of this description is based on the eyewitness experience of the author. See Vinson Synan, "The New Canterbury Tales" *The Pentecostal Holiness Advocate*, October 22, 1978, 12. Also see Michael Harper, ed., *A New Canterbury Tale: The Reports of the Anglican International Conference on Spiritual Renewal*

Held at Canterbury, July 19, 1978 (Bromcote, Nottinghamshire, 1978), 33 p.

18. Bob Slosser, *Miracle in Darien* (Plainfield, N.J., 1979), 268 p.

19. Beth Spring, "Spiritual Renewal Brings Booming Growth to Three Episcopal Churches in Northern Virginia," *Christianity Today*, January 13, 1984, 38-39.

CHAPTER 8
The Foursquare Church

1. Sources for Aimee Semple McPherson's life and ministry include her autobiography, *In the Service of the King* (New York, 1927), 316 p.; and *The Story of My Life* (Los Angeles, 1951), 50 p. Critical works include Robert P. Shuler's *McPhersonism* (Los Angeles, 192-) 63 p.; and Lately Thomas, *The Vanishing Evangelist* (New York: The Viking Press, 1959), 334 p.

2. McPherson, *The Story of My Life*, 15-79.

3. McPherson, *The Personal Testimony of Aimee Semple McPherson* (Los Angeles, 1984), 34-40; *Facts You Should Know Concerning the International Church of the Foursquare Gospel* (Los Angeles, 1983), 1-2.

4. See *Historical Data of the International Church of the Foursquare Gospel* (April 1968), 1.

5. McPherson, *Personal Testimony*, 41-46.

6. Ibid., 44-45.

7. Synan, *Holiness-Pentecostal Movement*, 198-199.

8. *Facts You Should Know About the International Church of the Foursquare Gospel*, 5; Harold Helms, personal interview with the author, Los Angeles, November 19, 1986.

9. McPherson, *Personal Testimony*, 47-49; Thomas, *Vanishing Evangelist*, 1-319.

10. *Articles of Incorporation and By-laws of the International Church of the Foursquare Gospel* (1986 edition), (Los Angeles, 1986), 20-28.

11. *Facts You Should Know*, 6; Aimee Semple McPherson, *This We Believe* (Los Angeles, n.d.), 7-35.

12. McPherson, *Story of My Life*, 75-142; *Personal Testimony*, 43.

13. See the *Articles of Incorporation*, 20-28.

14. *Yearbook, 1986, International Church of the Foursquare Gospel* (Los Angeles), 9.

15. Guy Duffield and Nathaniel Van Cleave, *Foundations of Pentecostal Theology* (Los Angeles, 1983), 624 p.

16. Harold Helms, personal interview with the author, Oklahoma City, Okla., November 19, 1986.

17. *(Foursquare) Yearbook, 1986*, 9.

18. Ibid., 1.

19. Ibid., 78-85.

20. Harold Helms, Synan interview.

CHAPTER 9
The Lutheran Renewal

1. Harald Bredesen, *Yes, Lord* (Plainfield, N.J., 1972), 48-57.

2. See *Time* magazine, March 29, 1963, 52.

Notes

3. Pat Robertson, *Shout It From the Housetops* (Plainfield, N.J., 1972), 65-79.

4. Larry Christenson, personal interview with the author, New Orleans, April 1, 1986. See also Christenson, *The Charismatic Renewal Among Lutherans* (Minneapolis, 1975) and Erling Jorstad, *Bold in the Spirit: Lutheran Charismatic Renewal in America Today* (Minneapolis, 1974). For Christenson's testimony, see "A Lutheran Pastor Speaks," *Trinity*, (Whitsuntide, 1962), 32-35.

5. For a brief treatment of Luther's view on the charismata, see Synan, *In the Latter Days*, 29-30.

6. Christenson, *Charismatic Renewal Among Lutherans*, 13-31.

7. Herbert Mjorud, personal interview with the author, Pittsburgh, Pa., May 21, 1986.

8. John P. Kildahl, *The Psychology of Speaking in Tongues* (New York, 1972). For early Lutheran official reports on Lutheran Pentecostalism, see McDonnell, *Presence, Power, Praise*, I, 21-566.

9. Larry Christenson, Synan interview.

10. Donald Pfotenhauer, personal interview with the author, Minneapolis, August 8, 1986. See the *Minneapolis Tribune*, February 4, 1968, 14 A.

11. News reports of the 1972 conference were carried by the *Minneapolis Star* in an article by Willmar Thorkelson, "God's Electricity Is Here," August 10, 1972, 1-3. Also Norris Wogen, personal interview with the author, Pittsburgh, Pa., May 20, 1986.

12. Christenson, *Charismatic Renewal Among Lutherans*, 46-52. See Christenson's *Welcome, Holy Spirit* (Minneapolis: 1987). Also see Theodore Jungkuntz, *Confirmation and the Charismata* (Lanham, Md.: University Press of America, 1983). These books are available at the Lutheran International Renewal Center in Minneapolis.

13. McDonnell, *Presence, Power, Praise*, I, 321-373.

14. Ibid., 369-373.

15. Ibid., 543-566.

16. Dennis Pederson, "Introducing...International Lutheran Center for Church Renewal," *Lutheran Renewal International*, Spring 1980, 14-17.

17. Larry Christenson, Synan interview.

18. Kenneth Kantzer, "The Charismatics Among Us," *Christianity Today*, February 22, 1980, 25-29.

19. C. Peter Wagner, "Survey of the Growth of the Charismatic Renewal" (Unpublished report, 1985).

20. Herbert Mirly, personal interview with the author, Charlotte, N.C., May 17, 1986 (Unpublished history and letter).

CHAPTER 10
The Mennonite Renewal

1. Derstine's story is told in his autobiography, *Following the Fire*, as told to Joanne Derstine (Plainfield, N.J., 1980).

2. Ibid., 83-93, 113-155. Gerald Derstine, personal interview with the author, Bradenton, Fla., January 4, 1986.

3. Derstine, *Following the Fire*, 165-174.

4. Ibid., 175-271. Also see "Champion of the Faith, Henry M. Brunk

1895-1985." (Bradenton, Fla., 1985), 6 p.

5. See Cornelius J. Dyck, ed., *An Introduction to Mennonite History* (Scottsdale, Pa., 1967), 324 p.; G.H. Williams, *The Radical Reformation*, (Philadelphia, 1962); and J.C. Wenger, *The Mennonite Church in America* (Scottsdale, Pa., 1966), 384 p.

6. Terry Miller, "Renewing the Anabaptist Vision," *Empowered*, Fall 1984, 8-9.

7. Roy Koch, *My Personal Pentecost* (Scottsdale, Pa., 1977), 15-35.

8. Nelson Litwiller, "Revitalized Retirement," in Koch, *My Personal Pentecost*, 110-111.

9. Ibid., 106-117.

10. Ibid., 118-275. Also see George R. Brunk II, ed., *Encounter With the Holy Spirit* (Scottsdale, Pa., 1972); and Bishop Elam Glick, "My Personal Pilgrimage" (Unpublished testimony).

11. McDonnell, *Presence, Power, Praise*, I, 285-287.

12. Ibid., II, 325-344.

13. Roy Koch, personal interview with the author, Charlotte, N.C., January 16, 1986. "Mennonite Renewal Services Formed," *Mennonite Renewal Newsletter*, February 1976, 1.

14. Ibid., October 1976, 1-2.

15. Miller, "Renewing the Anabaptist Vision," 9.

16. Roy Koch, "The Hopewell Mennonite Church" (Unpublished manuscript).

17. Koch, Synan interview.

18. Derstine, Synan interview.

19. See *Mennonite Renewal Services, Instrument for Renewal* (Brochure, 1986), 3 p.

CHAPTER 11
The Methodist Renewal

1. The standard early biography of Wesley is Robert Southey's *The Life of John Wesley*, 2 vols. (London, 1820). The most recent edition of his journal, letters and sermons is found in Thomas Jackson, ed., *The Works of John Wesley* (Grand Rapids, Mich., 1959), 14 vols.

2. See John Leland Peters, *Christian Perfection and American Methodism* (New York, 1956), 19-20; and Synan, *Holiness-Pentecostal Movement*, 13-32.

3. The definitive history of American Methodism is Emory Stevens Bucke, et al., *History of American Methodism*, 3 vols. (Nashville: Abingdon Press, 1964). Other popular histories include William Warren Sweet, *Methodism in American History* (New York, 1933); and Charles Ferguson, *Organizing to Beat the Devil, Methodists and the Making of America* (Garden City, N.Y., 1971).

4. See Ferguson, *Organizing to Beat the Devil*, 127-137; Bernard Weisberger, *They Gathered at the River* (New York, 1958), 20-25; Synan, *Holiness-Pentecostal Movement*, 21-25.

5. Timothy Smith, *Revivalism and Social Reform* (New York, 1957), 123-144.

6. Delbert Rose, *A Theology of Christian Experience* (Minneapolis, 1965), 23-78; Charles Edwin Jones, *Perfectionist Persuasion* (Metuchen, N.J., 1974), 16-21.

7. Donald Dayton, "From Christian Perfection to the Baptism of the Holy Spirit," In Synan, *Aspects of Pentecostal/Charismatic Origins*, 39-54

Notes

8. Timothy Smith, *Called Unto Holiness* (Kansas City, 1962), 150-204; Synan, *Holiness-Pentecostal Movement*, 37-76.

9. See "An Interview With Tommy Tyson, Evangelist," *Your Church*, November/December 1973, 10-28.

10. Ibid.

11. Ibid.

12. For the Oral Roberts University story, see David Edwin Harrell Jr., *Oral Roberts, An American Life* (Bloomington, Ind., 1985), 207-252.

13. Ibid. For Roberts' career in the Pentecostal Holiness Church, see Synan, *Old-Time Power*, 202-274.

14. Ibid., 263-268; Harrell, *Oral Roberts*, 287-311.

15. Ross Whetstone, personal interview with the author, Oklahoma City, Okla., September 25, 1986.

16. Ibid.

17. Ibid.; "Where Have We Been and Where Are We Going?" *Manna Ministries (UMRSF) Notes*, June 1985, 1-2.

18. See "Manna Ministries Moving Toward New Models of Service," *Manna Ministries (UMRSF) Notes*, May 1986, 1-2.

19. McDonnell, *Presence, Power, Praise*, II, 270-290.

20. Willis C. Hoover, *Historia Del Avivamiento Pentecostal de Chile* (Valparaiso, Chile, 1948); Synan, *In the Latter Days*, 57-62; C. Peter Wagner, *Look Out! The Pentecostals Are Coming* (Carol Stream, Ill., 1973), 16-18.

21. Javier Vasquez, personal interview with the author, Santiago, Chile, March 15, 1986.

22. Ross Whetstone, Synan interview and letter.

CHAPTER 12
The Orthodox Renewal

1. See Donald Attwater, *The Christian Churches of the East*, 2nd rev. ed., 2 vols. (Milwaukee, 1961-62).

2. Athanasios F.S. Emmert, "Charismatic Developments in the Eastern Orthodox Church," in Russell Spittler, *Perspectives on the New Pentecostalism* (Grand Rapids, Mich., 1976), 28-42.

3. Ed Plowman, "Mission to Orthodoxy: the Full Gospel," *Christianity Today*, April 26, 1974, 44-45; Eusebius Stephanou, *Charismatic Renewal in the Orthodox Church* (Fort Wayne, Ind., 1976).

4. Plowman, "Mission to Orthodoxy," 44. For Stephanou's perspective on renewal, see his "The Baptism in the Holy Spirit: An Orthodox Approach," *The Logos*, March-April 1983, 8-15; and "Pentecost and the Temple," *The Logos*, November-December 1984, 8-15.

5. William Hollar, "The Charismatic Renewal in the Eastern Orthodox Church in the United States of America With Emphasis on the Logos Ministry for Orthodox Renewal" (M.A. thesis, Concordia Theological Seminary, Fort Wayne, Ind.).

6. Bradley Nassif, "Greek Orthodox Church Tries to Muzzle a Popular Charismatic Priest," *Christianity Today*, November 25, 1983, 53. Also see Stephanou's "Sharing the Spirit," *The Logos*, March-April 1983, 3-5; and "Who Is Really Troubling Israel?," *The Logos*, May-June 1986, 1-3.

7. Gerald Munk, personal interview with the author, Glencoe, Mo., May 8, 1986. Also see "1978 Continental Conference on the Charismatic Renewal in the Orthodox Church," *Theosis*, June 1978, 7.

CHAPTER 13
The Pentecostal Holiness Church

1. The two standard histories of the church are Joseph E. Campbell, *The Pentecostal Holiness Church, 1898-1948* (Franklin Springs, Ga., 1951), 537 p.; and Vinson Synan, *The Old-Time Power: A History of the Pentecostal Holiness Church* (Franklin Springs, Ga., 1971), 239 p. Also useful is A.D. Beacham Jr.'s *A Brief History of the Pentecostal Holiness Church* (Franklin Springs, Ga., 1983), 123 p.; and Harold Paul's *From Printer's Devil to Bishop* (Franklin Springs, Ga., 1976), 177 p.

2. Synan, *Old-Time Power*, 107.

3. Ibid., 103-110.

4. Joseph H. King, *Yet Speaketh, The Memoirs of the Late Bishop Joseph H. King* (Franklin Springs, Ga., 1949), 111-121.

5. Synan, *Holiness-Pentecostal Movement*, 117-139.

6. Campbell, *Pentecostal Holiness Church, 1898-1948*, 239-253.

7. N.J. Holmes, *Life Sketches and Sermons* (Franklin Springs, Ga., 1920), 135-148.

8. Campbell, *Pentecostal Holiness Church, 1898-1948*, 254-269; Beacham, *A Brief History*, 55.

9. G.F. Taylor, *The Spirit and the Bride* (Dunn, N.C., 1907), 175 p.; Joseph H. King, *From Passover to Pentecost* (Memphis, Tenn., 1914), 182 p.

10. See Synan, *Holiness-Pentecostal Movement*, 141-163.

11. Synan, *Old-Time Power*, 165-171.

12. Ibid., 265-268. Also see David Harrell Jr.'s *Oral Roberts: An American Life*, 8-55, 287-311.

13. Synan, *Old-Time Power*, 225-228.

14. Ibid., 266-267.

15. See *Minutes of the Twentieth General Conference of the Pentecostal Holiness Church, Inc.* (Franklin Springs, Ga., 1985), 92-99.

CHAPTER 14
The Presbyterian and Reformed Renewal

1. John Calvin, *Institutes of the Christian Religion*, John T. McNeill, ed., 4 vols. (Philadelphia, 1960), Vol. I, 15-31; IV, 1466-1484. Also see Calvin's *New Testament Commentaries: 1 Corinthians* (Grand Rapids, Mich., 1960), 258-273.

2. Benjamin B. Warfield, *Counterfeit Miracles* (Carlisle, Pa., 1918). Also see Ronald A. Knox, *Enthusiasm* (London: Clarendon Press, 1950).

3. See Bernard Weisberger, *They Gathered at the River* (New York, 1958), 20-25, and Archie Robertson, *That Old-Time Religion* (Boston, 1950), 56-57.

4. Jonathan Edwards, *A Faithful Narrative of the Surprising Work of God* (1737); and *The Distinguishing Marks of a Work of the Spirit of God* (1741). This awakening is discussed in Richard Lovelace, *Dynamics of Spiritual Life* (Downers Grove, Ill., 1979), 35-46.

Notes

5. Synan, *In the Latter Days*, 25, 37, 52; Smith, *Revivalism and Social Reform*, 114-134.

6. See William S. Merricks, *Edward Irving, The Forgotten Giant* (East Peoria, Ill., 1983), 179-180.

7. Holmes, *Life Sketches and Sermons*, 9-97.

8. James H. Brown, personal interview with the author, Charlotte, N.C., March 5, 1986. Also letter from Brown to Synan, January 27, 1986.

9. George "Brick" Bradford, personal interview with the author, Oklahoma City, Okla., December 6, 1985.

10. Ibid.; "Charismatic Renewal in the Reformed Tradition," *Renewal News*, May-June 1981, 1-4.

11. Whitaker's story is given in his booklet, *Hang in There: Counsel for Charismatics* (Plainfield, N.J., 1974), 38-41.

12. Brick Bradford, Synan interview. Letter from Whitaker to the author, December 19, 1985. The records of the case, *The Reverend Robert C. Whitaker, Complainant vs. The Synod of Arizona, United Presbyterian Church in the United States of America, Respondent*, may be found in the office of the Presbyterian and Reformed Renewal Ministries offices in Oklahoma City.

13. This report is published in McDonnell's *Presence, Power, and Praise*, I, 221-282. (The 1971 report of the Presbyterian Church in the United States is published on 287-317.)

14. See Catherine Marshall, *Something More* (New York, 1974); Quebedeaux, *The New Charismatics II*, 131, 133-134.

15. Ibid., 133, 146-147, 161. See J. Rodman Williams, *The Pentecostal Reality* (Plainfield, N.J., 1972), and *The Era of the Spirit* (Plainfield, N.J., 1971).

16. "Presbyterian Charismatic Communion Changes Name to Presbyterian and Reformed Renewal Ministries International," *Renewal News*, May-June 1984, 1-3.

17. Brick Bradford, Synan interview.

18. Ibid.

CHAPTER 15
The United Church of Christ Renewal

1. For the story of the Puritans in England and America, see Alan Simpson, *Puritanism in Old and New England* (Chicago, 1955). For the best scholarly treatment of New England Puritanism see the works of Perry Miller, especially his two volume *The New England Mind* (New York: The McMillan Company, 1961). Also helpful is Carl Degler's *Out of Our Past: The Forces That Shaped Modern America* (New York, 1970). A Christian interpretation is given in Peter Marshall and David Manuel, *The Light and the Glory* (Old Tappan, N.J., 1977), 106-209.

2. The standard denominational history for the United Church of Christ is Douglas Horton, *The United Church of Christ: Its Origins, Organization & Role in the World Today* (New York, 1962). Also see Barbara Brown Zickmund, *Hidden Histories in the United Church of Christ* (New York, 1984).

3. A succinct history is given in *About the United Church of Christ, A Guide to More Effective Church Membership* (South Deerfield, Mass., 1980), 15 p.

4. George Allen, "The United Church of Christ: A Pluralistic Church or a Liberal One," in *Focus Newsletter*, August 1982, 7-8.

5. See Gerald M. Sanders, *An Introduction to the Biblical Witness Fellowship* (Knoxville, Tenn., 1984), 6 p.; and *The Spiritual Development Network of the United Church of Christ* (Berkeley, Calif., 1986), 4 p. Also helpful are *The Witness of the Biblical Witness Fellowship: A Confessing Movement Within the U.C.C.*, August 1986, 1-8; and George Allen, "UCC Churches on the Move/What I've Learned About Reviving the Church," *Living Faith*, Winter 1981, 22-27. A program for renewal inspired by Jonathan Edwards and other Puritan divines is given by Richard Lovelace in his *Dynamics of Spiritual Life*.

6. Vernon Stoop, personal interviews, letters and notes to the author, July 8, 1986, and July 18, 1986.

7. Robert K. Arakaki, "The Holy Spirit and the United Church of Christ," *Focus Newsletter*, May 1983, 1-4; see Vernon Stoop, *Fellowship of Charismatic Christians in the United Church of Christ* (Sassamansville, Pa., n.d.), 1-2.

8. Stoop, letters, notes and Synan interview.

9. Ibid.

10. Ibid.

11. Ibid. Also see *What Is the Fellowship of Charismatic Christians in the United Church of Christ?* (Sassamansville, Pa., n.d.), 6 p.

12. Stoop, letters, notes and Synan interview.

13. Ibid.

14. Ibid.

CHAPTER 16
The Wesleyan Charismatics

1. The historic connection between the Holiness and Pentecostal Movements is traced in Synan's *Holiness-Pentecostal Movement*, 13-140.

2. Ibid., 141-163.

3. Timothy Smith, *Called Unto Holiness* (Kansas City, 1962), 316-319; M.E. Redford, *The Rise of the Church of the Nazarene* (Kansas City: Nazarene Publishing House, 1951), 39-42; Phineas Bresee, "The Gift of Tongues," *Nazarene Messenger*, December 13, 1906, 6. This is reprinted in Vinson Synan, *Azusa Street* (Plainfield, N.J., 1980), 182-184.

4. Smith, *Called Unto Holiness*, 118; Alma White, *Demons and Tongues* (Zarephath, N.J., 1949); Jones, *The Perfectionist Persuasion*, 121, 173.

5. Synan, *Holiness-Pentecostal Movement*, 117-139.

6. John L. Peters, personal interview with the author, Oklahoma City, Okla., December 10, 1986.

7. Warren Black, personal interview with the author, Cincinnati, Ohio, September 29, 1986. See also Warren Black, "A New Dimension," in *The Acts of the Holy Spirit Among the Nazarenes Today* (Los Angeles, 1973), 23-29.

8. Warren Black, Synan interview.

9. See the Judicial Report No. 3, containing memorials from West Virginia, Ohio and Illinois (from the 1972 General Assembly which met in Miami, Florida). For the Calvary Holiness Church merger story, see Jack Ford, *In the Steps of John Wesley* (Kansas City, 1968), 171-174.

10. See the *Journal of the Nineteenth General Assembly of the Church of the Nazarene*, 240; and McDonnell, *Presence, Power, and Praise*, I, 220-221.

Notes

11. Dan Brady, personal interview with the author, Cincinnati, Ohio, July 14, 1986. See Dan Brady, "Continuing in Tongues" (Unpublished manuscript, 1986), 20 p.

12. See "Evidence of the Baptism With the Holy Spirit," in the *Manual/1985 Church of the Nazarene* (Kansas City, 1985), 284.

13. Wilbur Jackson, personal interview with the author, Cincinnati, Ohio, September 28, 1986.

14. See the "Report: Study Committee on Glossolalia" (presented to the general assembly of the Church of God, June 18, 1986), 9 p.; Paul Tanner, personal interview with the author, Oklahoma City, Okla., July 21, 1986.

15. See *Acts of the Holy Spirit Among the Nazarenes Today*, 9-72.

16. Ibid., 9-17.

17. See the *Wesleyan Holiness Charismatic Fellowship Newsletter* (Athens, Ga., n.d.), 4 p.; Wilbur Jackson, Synan interview.

18. Howard Snyder, *The Divided Flame: Wesleyans and the Charismatic Renewal* (Grand Rapids, Mich., 1986), 120 p.

Bibliography

Primary Sources

Bartleman, Frank, *How "Pentecost" Came to Los Angeles*. Los Angeles: Privately printed, 1925. Reprinted with introduction and appendices by Vinson Synan and Logos Publications in Plainfield, N.J., in 1980 under the title *Azusa Street*.

Bayley, Robert, *The Healing Ministry of the Local Church*. Oklahoma City: Presbyterian Charismatic Communion, 1983.

Bennett, Dennis, *Nine O'Clock in the Morning*. Plainfield, N.J.: Logos Press, 1970.

Boone, Pat, *A New Song*. Carol Stream, Ill.: Creation House, 1970.

Bradford, Brick, *Releasing the Power of the Holy Spirit*. Oklahoma City: Presbyterian Charismatic Communion, 1983.

Bredesen, Harald, *Yes, Lord*. Plainfield, N.J.: Logos International, 1972.

Brumback, Carl, *God in Three Persons*. Cleveland, Tenn.: Pathway Press, 1959.

Brunk, George R. II, ed. *Encounter With the Holy Spirit*. Scottsdale, Pa.: Herald Press, 1972.

Calvin, John, *Institutes of the Christian Religion*, 4 vols. John T. McNeill, ed. Philadelphia: The Westminster Press, 1960.

Calvin, John, *New Testament Commentaries: 1 Corinthians*. Grand Rapids, Mich.: Wm. B. Eerdmans Company, 1960.

Christenson, Larry, et al., *Welcome, Holy Spirit*. Minneapolis: Augsburg Publishing House, 1987.

Derstine, Gerald, *Following the Fire*, as told to Joanne Derstine. Plainfield, N.J.: Logos International, 1980.

Duffield, Guy, and Nathaniel van Cleave, *Foundations of Pentecostal Theology*. Los Angeles: L.I.F.E. Bible College, 1983.

THE 20TH-CENTURY PENTECOSTAL EXPLOSION

Du Plessis, David, *A Man Called Mr. Pentecost: David du Plessis*, as told to Bob Slosser. Plainfield, N.J.: Logos International, 1977.

————. *The Spirit Bade Me Go*, rev. ed. Plainfield, N.J.: Logos International, 1977.

Ervin, Howard, *These Are Not Drunken as Ye Suppose*. Plainfield, N.J.: Logos International, 1967.

Gelpi, Donald, *Pentecostalism: A Theological Viewpoint*. New York: Paulist Press, 1971.

Gordon, A.J., *The Ministry of Healing, Miracles of Cure in All Ages*. Harrisburg, Penn.: Christian Publications, 1961.

Harper, Michael, *A New Canterbury Tale: The Reports of the Anglican International Conference on Spiritual Renewal Held at Canterbury, July 19, 1978*. Bromcote, Nottinghamshire: Grove Books, 1978.

————. *Three Sisters*. Wheaton, Ill.: Tyndale Publishers Inc., 1979.

Hiscox, Edward T., *The New Directory for Baptist Churches*. Philadelphia: The Judson Press, 1984.

Holmes, N.J., *Life Sketches and Sermons*. Franklin Springs, Ga.: Publishing House of the Pentecostal Holiness Church, 1920.

Hoover, Willis C., *Historia del Avivamiento Pentecostal en Chile*. Valparaiso: 1948.

Jackson, Thomas, ed., *The Works of John Wesley*, 14 vols. Grand Rapids, Mich.: Zondervan Publishing House, 1959.

Jungkuntz, Theodore, *Confirmation and the Charismata*. Lanham, Md.: University Press of America, 1983.

King, Joseph H., *Yet Speaketh, the Memoirs of the Late Bishop Joseph H. King*. Franklin Springs, Ga.: Publishing House of the Pentecostal Holiness Church, 1949.

Koch, Roy, *My Personal Pentecost*. Scottsdale, Pa.: Herald Press, 1984.

Lawson, J. Gilchrist, *Deeper Experiences of Famous Christians*. Anderson, Ind.: Gospel Trumpet Company, 1911.

Lindsell, Harold, *The Holy Spirit in the Latter Days*. Nashville: Thomas Nelson, 1983.

Lumpkin, W.L., *Baptist Confessions of Faith*. Chicago: Judson Press, 1959.

Manuel, David, *Like a Mighty River: A Personal Account of the Charismatic Conference of 1977*. Orleans, Mass.: Rock Harbor Press, 1977.

Marshall, Catherine, *Something More*. New York: McGraw-Hill, 1974.

Mason, Charles Harrison, *The History and Life of Elder C.H. Mason*. Memphis: Howe Printing Department, 1920.

McDonnell, Kilian, and Arnold Bittlinger, *The Baptism in the Holy Spirit as an Ecumenical Problem*. South Bend, Ind.: Charismatic Renewal Services, 1972.

McDonnell, Kilian, *Catholic Pentecostalism: Problems in Evaluation*. Pecos, N.M.: Dove Publications, 1970.

McPherson, Aimee Semple, *In the Service of the King*. New York: Boni and Liverwright, 1927.

Bibliography

————. *The Personal Testimony of Aimee Semple McPherson*. Los Angeles: Starling Press, 1984.

————. *The Story of My Life*. Los Angeles: Echo Park Evangelistic Associates, 1951.

————. *This We Believe*. Los Angeles: 1983.

O'Connor, Edward, *The Pentecostal Movement in the Catholic Church*. Notre Dame, Ind.: Ave Maria Press, 1971.

Patterson, J.O., et al., *History and Formative Years of the Church of God in Christ With Excerpts From the Life and Works of Bishop C.H. Mason*. Memphis: Church of God in Christ Publishing House, 1969.

Pope, Liston, *Millhands and Preachers, A Study of Gastonia*. New Haven: Yale University Press, 1946.

Pursey, Barbara A., *Charismatic Renewal and You*. Oklahoma City: Presbyterian Renewal Publications, 1987.

————. *The Gifts of the Holy Spirit*. Oklahoma City: Presbyterian and Reformed Renewal Ministries, 1984.

Ranaghan, Kevin and Dorothy, *Catholic Pentecostals*. New York: Paulist Press, 1969.

Robertson, Pat, *Shout It From the Housetops*. Plainfield, N.J.: Logos International, 1972.

Sanders, Gerald M., *An Introduction to the Biblical Witness Fellowship*. Knoxville, Tenn.: 1984.

Shakarian, Demos, *The Happiest People on Earth*. Old Tappan, N.J.: Chosen Books, 1975.

Sherrill, John, *They Speak With Other Tongues*. New York: McGraw-Hill, 1964.

Shuler, Robert P., *McPhersonism*. Los Angeles, 192-.

Simpson, A.B., *The Holy Spirit, or Power From on High*. Harrisburg, Penn.: Christian Publications Inc., 1896.

Slosser, Bob, *Miracle in Darien*. Plainfield, N.J.: Logos International, 1979.

Snyder, Howard, *The Divided Flame: Wesleyans and the Charismatic Renewal*. Grand Rapids: Francis Asbury Press, 1986.

Spurgeon, Charles Haddon, *Spurgeon's Sermons*. Grand Rapids: Zondervan reprint from 1857.

Stephanou, Eusebius, *Charismatic Renewal in the Orthodox Church*. Fort Wayne, Ind.: Logos Ministries for Orthodox Renewal, 1976.

Stone, Barton, *The Biography of Eld. Barton Stone, Written by Himself With Additions and Reflections*. Cincinnati: J.A. and U.P. James, 1847.

Stone, Jean, and Harald Bredesen, *The Charismatic Renewal in the Historic Churches*. Van Nuys, Calif.: Blessed Trinity Society, 1963.

Stoop, Vernon, *Fellowship of Charismatic Christians in the United Church of Christ*. Sassamansville, Penn.: (n.d.).

————. *What Is the Fellowship of Charismatic Christians in the United Church of Christ?*. Sassamansville, Penn.: (n.d.).

Suenens, Leon Joseph Cardinal, *A New Pentecost?*. New York: Seabury Press, 1974.

Synan, Vinson, *Charismatic Bridges*. Ann Arbor: Word of Life, 1974.

Taylor, George F., *The Spirit and the Bride*. Dunn, N.C.: Private printing, 1907.

Tomlinson, A.J., *Answering the Call of God*. Cleveland, Tenn.: White Wing Publishing House, 1942.

Tomlinson, Homer, *The Shout of a King*. New York: The Church of God, World Headquarters, 1965.

————. ed., *Diary of A.J. Tomlinson, 1901-1923*. New York: The Ryder Press, 1949.

Torbet, R.G., *A History of the Baptists*, rev. ed. Philadelphia: Judson Press, 1963.

Underwood, A.C., *A History of the English Baptists*. London: Baptist Union Publishing Department, 1947.

Van Ness, I.J., *The Baptist Spirit*. Nashville: Sunday School Board of the Southern Baptist Convention, 1914.

Warfield, Benjamin B., *Counterfeit Miracles*. Carlisle, Pa.: The Banner of Truth Trust, 1918.

————. *Miracles: Yesterday and Today*. Grand Rapids, Mich.: Wm. B. Eerdmans Publishing Co., 1954.

Wells, David, *Revolution in Rome*. Downer's Grove, Ill.: Intervarsity Press, 1972.

Whitaker, Robert, *Hang in There: Counsel for Charismatics*. Plainfield, N.J.: Logos International, 1974.

White, Alma, *Demons and Tongues*. Bound Brook, N.J.: The Pentecostal Union, 1910.

Wilkerson, David, *The Cross and the Switchblade*. New York: Random House, 1963.

Williams, J. Rodman, *The Era of the Spirit*. Plainfield, N.J.: Logos International, 1971.

————. *The Pentecostal Reality*. Plainfield, N.J.: Logos International, 1972.

Secondary Sources

Anderson, Robert Mapes, *Vision of the Disinherited: The Making of American Pentecostalism*. New York: Oxford University Press, 1979.

Attwater, Donald, *The Christian Churches of the East*, 2nd rev. ed., 2 vols. Milwaukee: Bruce Publishing Company, 1961-1962.

Beacham, A.D. Jr., *A Brief History of the Pentecostal Holiness Church*. Franklin Springs, Ga.: Advocate Press, 1983.

Blumhofer, Edith Waldvogel, *The Assemblies of God: A Popular History*. Springfield, Mo.: Gospel Publishing House, 1985.

Brumback, Carl, *Suddenly...From Heaven: A History of the Assemblies of God*. Springfield, Mo.: Gospel Publishing House, 1961.

Bibliography

Bucke, Emory Stevens, et al., *History of American Methodism*, 3 vols. Nashville: Abingdon Press, 1964.

Campbell, Joseph E., *The Pentecostal Holiness Church, 1898-1948*. Franklin Springs, Ga.: Publishing House of the Pentecostal Holiness Church, 1951.

Christenson, Larry, *A Message to the Charismatic Movement*. Weymouth, Mass.: Dimension, 1972.

—————. *The Charismatic Renewal Among Lutherans*. Minneapolis: Lutheran Charismatic Renewal Services, 1975.

Cobbins, Otho B., *History of the Church of Christ (Holiness) U.S.A*. New York: Vantage Press, 1966.

Conn, Charles W., *Like a Mighty Army Moves the Church of God*. Cleveland, Tenn.: Church of God Publishing House, 1955.

—————. *Where the Saints Have Trod*. Cleveland, Tenn.: Church of God Publishing House, 1959.

Davidson, Charles, *Upon This Rock*, 3 vols. Cleveland, Tenn.: White Wing Publishing House, 1973-1976.

Degler, Carl, *Out of Our Past: The Forces That Shaped Modern America*. New York: Harper & Row Publishers, 1970.

Dieter, Melvin, *The Holiness Revival of the Nineteenth Century*. Metuchen, N.J.: Scarecrow Press, 1980.

Duggar, Lillie, *A.J. Tomlinson, Former General Overseer of the Church of God*. Cleveland, Tenn.: White Wing Publishing House, 1964.

Durasoff, Steve, *Bright Wind of the Spirit*. New York: Prentice-Hall, 1972.

Dyck, Cornelius J., *An Introduction to Mennonite History*. Scottsdale, Penn.: Herald Press, 1967.

Ferguson, Charles, *Organizing to Beat the Devil: Methodists and the Making of America*. Garden City, N.Y.: Doubleday and Company, 1971.

Ford, Jack, *In the Steps of John Wesley*. Kansas City: Nazarene Publishing House, 1968.

Garrett, Leroy, *The Stone-Campbell Movement*. Joplin, Mo.: College Press Company, 1981.

Garrison, Ernest, and Alfred DeGroot, *The Disciples of Christ: A History*. St. Louis: Christian Board of Publications, 1958.

Garvin, Phillip, *Religious America*. New York: McGraw-Hill Book Company, 1974.

Harper, Michael, *As at the Beginning: The Twentieth-Century Pentecostal Revival*. London: Hodder and Stoughton, 1965.

Harrell, David Edwin Jr., *All Things Are Possible: The Healing and Charismatic Revivals in Modern America*. Bloomington, Ind.: Indiana University Press, 1975.

—————. *A Social History of the Disciples of Christ*, 2 vols. Nashville: Disciples of Christ Historical Society, 1966.

—————. *Oral Roberts, An American Life*. Bloomington, Ind.: University of Indiana Press, 1985.

Hollenweger, Walter, *The Pentecostals: The Charismatic Movement in the*

Churches. Minneapolis: Augsburg Press, 1972.

Horton, Douglas, *The United Church of Christ: Its Origins, Organization and Role in the World Today*. New York: Thomas Nelson Publishers, 1962.

Jorstad, Erling, *Bold in the Spirit: Lutheran Charismatic Renewal in America Today*. Minneapolis: Augsburg Publishing House, 1974.

Jones, Charles Edwin, *Perfectionist Persuasion*. Metuchen, N.J.: Scarecrow Press, 1974.

Kelsey, Morton, *Tongue Speaking: An Experiment in Spiritual Experience*. New York: Doubleday & Company, 1964.

Kendrick, Klaud, *The Promise Fulfilled: A History of the Assemblies of God*. Springfield, Mo.: Gospel Publishing House, 1961.

Kildahl, John P., *The Psychology of Speaking in Tongues*. New York: Harper & Row, 1972.

Lovelace, Richard, *Dynamics of Spiritual Life*. Downers Grove, Ill.: Intervarsity Press, 1979.

Marshall, Peter, and David Manuel, *The Light and the Glory*. Old Tappan, N.J.: Fleming H. Revell Company, 1977.

Menzies, William, *Anointed to Serve: The Story of the Assemblies of God*. Springfield, Mo.: Gospel Publishing House, 1971.

McDonnell, Kilian, *Charismatic Renewal and the Churches*. New York: The Seabury Press, 1976.

Merricks, William, *Edward Irving, the Forgotten Giant*. East Peoria, Ill.: Scribe's Chamber Publications, 1983.

Miller, Perry, *The New England Mind*, 2 vols. New York: The McMillan Company, 1961.

Nichols, John, *Pentecostalism*. New York: Harper & Row, 1966.

Orr, J. Edwin, *The Flaming Tongue: The Impact of the Twentieth-Century Revivals*. Chicago: Moody Press, 1973.

Parham, Sarah E., *The Life of Charles F. Parham*. Joplin, Mo.: Tri-State Printing Company, 1930.

Paul, Harold, *From Printer's Devil to Bishop*. Franklin Springs, Ga.: Advocate Press, 1976.

Peters, John Leland, *Christian Perfection and American Methodism*. New York: Abingdon Press, 1956.

Pope, Liston, *Millhands and Preachers: A Study of Gastonia*. New Haven: Yale University Press, 1946.

Post, Avery E., ed., *United Church of Christ: History and Program*. New York: United Church Press, 1982.

Quebedeaux, Richard, *The New Charismatics II: How a Christian Renewal Movement Became Part of the American Religious Mainstream*. San Francisco: Harper & Row Publishers, 1983.

Ranaghan, Kevin and Dorothy, *Catholic Pentecostals*. Paramus, N.J.: Paulist Press, 1969.

Bibliography

Redford, M.E., *The Rise of the Church of the Nazarene*. Kansas City: Nazarene Publishing House, 1951.

Root, Jean Christie, *Edward Irving: Man, Preacher, Prophet*. Boston: Sherman, French & Company, 1912.

Rose, Delbert, *A Theology of Christian Experience*. Minneapolis: Bethany Fellowship, Inc., 1965.

Sandeen, Ernest, *The Roots of Fundamentalism: British and American Millenarianism, 1800-1930*. Chicago: University of Chicago Press, 1970.

Simpson, Alan, *Puritanism in Old and New England*. Chicago: University of Chicago Press, 1955.

Smith, Timothy, *Called Unto Holiness*. Kansas City: Nazarene Publishing House, 1962.

——— . *Revivalism and Social Reform in Mid-Nineteenth Century America*. New York: Abingdon Press, 1957.

Southey, Robert, *The Life of John Wesley*. London: Longmans Hurst and Company, 1820.

Spittler, Russell, *Perspectives on the New Pentecostalism*. Grand Rapids, Mich.: Baker Book House, 1976.

Strachan, Gordon, *The Pentecostal Theology of Edward Irving*. London: Dartan, Longman & Todd, 1973.

Sullivan, Francis, C.S., *Charisms and Charismatic Renewal*. Ann Arbor, Mich.: Servant Books, 1982.

Sweet, William Warren, *Methodism in American History*. New York: Abingdon Press, 1933.

Synan, Vinson, ed., *Aspects of Pentecostal-Charismatic Origins*. Plainfield, N.J.: Logos International, 1975.

——— . *Charismatic Bridges*. Ann Arbor, Mich.: Word of Life, 1974.

——— . *The Holiness-Pentecostal Movement in the United States*. Grand Rapids, Mich.: Wm. B. Eerdmans Company, 1971.

——— . *In the Latter Days: The Outpouring of the Holy Spirit in the Twentieth Century*. Ann Arbor, Mich.: Servant Books, 1984.

——— . *The Old-Time Power: A History of the Pentecostal Holiness Church*. Franklin Springs, Ga.: Advocate Press, 1973.

Tucker, David M., *Black Pastors and Leaders: Memphis, 1819-1972*. Memphis: Memphis State University Press, 1975.

Thomas, Lately, *The Vanishing Evangelist*. New York: The Viking Press, 1959.

Vergara, Ignacio, *El Protestantismo en Chile*. Santiago: 1962.

Wagner, C. Peter, *Look Out! The Pentecostals Are Coming*. Carol Stream, Ill.: Creation House, 1973.

Weisberger, Bernard, *They Gathered at the River*. New York: Little, Brown, 1958.

West, William Garrett, *Barton Warren Stone: Early American Advocate of Christian Unity*. Nashville: Disciples of Christ Historical Society, 1954.

Williams, G.H., *The Radical Reformation*. Philadelphia: Westminster Press, 1962.

THE 20TH-CENTURY PENTECOSTAL EXPLOSION

Zickmund, Barbara Brown, *Hidden Histories in the United Church of Christ*. New York: Pilgrim Press, 1984.

Articles

"A Witness to Our Brothers and Sisters in the United Church of Christ From the Craigville III Theological Colloquy," *United Church News*, (December 1986), p. 14.

Allen, George, "The United Church of Christ: A Pluralistic Church or a Liberal One?" *Focus Newsletter*, (August 1982), pp. 7-8.

―――― . "UCC Churches on the Move/ What I've Learned About Reviving the Church," *Living Faith*, (Winter 1981), pp. 22-27.

Ambrose, George, "God Said It. I Believe It. That Settles It: Spiritual Renewal in the Church of Christ," *Charisma*, (July 1984), pp. 71-72.

Arakaki, Robert K., "The Holy Spirit and the United Church of Christ," *Focus Newsletter*, (May 1983), pp. 1-4.

Black, Warren, "A New Dimension," in *The Acts of the Holy Spirit Among the Nazarenes Today*. Los Angeles: Full Gospel Business Men's Fellowship International, 1973.

Bradford, Brick, "Charismatic Renewal in the Reformed Tradition," *Renewal News*, (May-June 1981), pp. 1-4.

―――― . "Presbyterian Charismatic Communion Changes Name to Presbyterian and Reformed Ministries International," *Renewal News*, (May-June 1984), pp. 1-3.

Bresee, Phineas, "The Gift of Tongues," *The Nazarene Messenger*, (December 13, 1906), p. 6.

Buckingham, Jamie, "The Music of Spiritual Awakening: Belmont Church of Christ," *Charisma*, (July 1984), pp. 32-37.

"But What About Hicks?," *Christian Century*, July 7, 1954, pp. 814-815.

Christenson, Larry, "A Lutheran Pastor Speaks," *Trinity*, (Whitsuntide, 1962), pp. 32-35.

Clark, Gary, "An Extra Dimension," *Christian Life*, (August 1985), pp. 36-39.

Davis, Arnor S., "The Pentecostal Movement in Black Christianity," *Black Church*, 2:1 (1972), pp. 65-88.

Dayton, Donald, "From Christian Perfection to the Baptism of the Holy Spirit," in Vinson Synan, *Aspects of Pentecostal Charismatics Origins*. Plainfield, N.J.: Logos International, 1975.

Duin, Julia, "Signs and Wonders in New Orleans," *Christianity Today*, (November 2, 1986), pp. 26-27.

Emmert, Athanasios, F.S., "Charismatic Developments in the Eastern Orthodox Church," in Russell Spittler, *Perspectives on the New Pentecostalism*. Grand Rapids, Mich.: Baker Book House, 1976.

Farrell, Frank, "Outburst of Tongues: The New Penetration," *Christianity*

222

Today, 7(September 13, 1963), 3-7.

Flower, J. Roswell, "Birth of the Pentecostal Movement," *The Pentecostal Evangel* (November 26, 1950), p. 3.

————. "History of the Assemblies of God." (n.p., n.d.)

Ghezzi, Bertil, "Three Charismatic Communities," in Kevin and Dorothy Ranaghan, *As the Spirit Leads Us*, New York: Paulist Press, 1971, pp. 164-186.

Houghey, John C., "The Holy Spirit: A Ghost No Longer," *America*, (June 16, 1973), p. 551.

Hughes, Ray, "A Traditional Pentecostal Looks at the New Pentecostals," *Christianity Today* 18(June 7, 1974), p. 6-10.

Jahr, Mary Ann, "A Turning Point," *New Covenant*, (August 1974), p. 4.

Kantzer, Kenneth, "The Charismatics Among Us," *Christianity Today* 24(February 22, 1980), 25-29.

Lawson, Steve, "Episcopal Renewal on the Move," *Charisma*, (March 1986), p. 64.

————. "Leaders Unite in New Orleans," *Charisma*, (December 1980), pp. 58-59.

Lilly, Fred, "Unity in Christ," *New Covenant*, (December 1986), pp. 12-13.

Litwiller, Nelson, "Revitalized Retirement," in Roy Koch, *My Personal Pentecost*. Scottsdale, Pa.: Herald Press, 1977.

Lovett, Leonard, "Black Origins of the Pentecostal Movement," in Vinson Synan, *Aspects of Pentecostal/Charismatic Origins*. Plainfield, N.J.: Logos International, 1975.

MacCollam, Joel A., "O Lord, We're Free at Last," *Charisma*, (October 1983), pp. 40-46.

Manney, James, "Father Michael Scanlan and the University of Steubenville," *New Covenant*, (September 1985), pp. 10-14.

Mansfield, Patti Gallagher, "Come, Holy Spirit," *New Covenant*, (February 1986), pp. 8-10.

"Mennonite Renewal Services Formed," *Mennonite Renewal Newsletter*, (February 1976), p. 1.

Miller, Terry, "Renewing the Anabaptist Vision," *Empowered*, (Fall 1984), pp. 8-9.

Nassif, Bradley, "Greek Orthodox Church Tries to Muzzle Popular Charismatic Priest," *Christianity Today*, (November 25, 1983), p. 53.

O'Connor, Edward, "The Hidden Roots of the Charismatic Renewal in the Catholic Church," in Vinson Synan, *Aspects of Pentecostal/Charismatic Origins*. Plainfield, N.J.: Logos International, 1975, pp. 169-192.

Pederson, Dennis, "Introducing...International Lutheran Center for Church Renewal," *Lutheran Renewal International*, (Spring 1980), pp. 14-17.

Plowman, Edward, "Mission to Orthodoxy, The Full Gospel," *Christianity Today*, (April 26, 1974), pp. 44-45.

Robison, James, "Restoration Report," *Days of Restoration*, (May-June 1986), pp. 11-13.

Robinson, Ras, "Who Are You Who Read *Fulness*?," *Fulness Magazine*, (July-

August 1986), p. 4.

Rose, Bruce L., "Episcopal Church: Catholic-Evangelical-Charismatic," *Acts 29*, (February 1984), pp. 1-6.

Smith, Tom, "Welcome to Conference '86," *Paraclete Journal*, (July 1986), p. 2.

Spring, Beth, "Spiritual Renewal Brings Booming Church Growth to Three Episcopal Churches in Northern Virginia," *Christianity Today*, (January 13, 1984), pp. 38-39.

Stephanou, Eusebius, "The Baptism in the Holy Spirit, An Orthodox Approach," *The Logos*, (March-April 1983), pp. 8-15.

————. "Pentecost and the Temple," *The Logos*, (November-December 1984), pp. 8-10.

————. "Sharing the Spirit," *The Logos*, (March-April 1983), pp. 3-5.

————. "Who Is Really Troubling Israel?" *The Logos*, (May-June 1986), pp. 1-3.

Synan, Vinson, "The New Canterbury Tales," *The Pentecostal Holiness Advocate*, (October 10, 1978), p. 12.

Thorkelson, Willmar, "God's Electricity Is Here," *Minneapolis Star*, (August 10, 1972), pp. 1-3.

Tinney, James, "Black Pentecostals Convene," *Christianity Today*, (December 4, 1970), p. 36.

————. "Black Pentecostals Setting Up the Kingdom," *Christianity Today*, (December 5, 1975), pp 42-43.

Van Dusen, Henry P., "Third Force in Christendom," *Life*, (June 9, 1958), pp. 113-124.

Wagner, C. Peter, "A Third Wave?," *Pastoral Renewal*, (July-August 1983), pp. 1-5.

Whetstone, Ross, "Manna Ministries Moving Toward New Models of Service," *Manna Ministries (UMRSF) Notes*, (May 1986), pp. 1-2.

————. "Where Have We Been and Where Are We Going?," *Manna Ministries (UMRSF) Notes*, (June 1985), pp. 1-2.

Whitten, Clark, "Profile in Grace," *Fulness Magazine*, (July-August 1986), pp. 9-11.

Collections, Brochures, Minutes and Unpublished Materials

About the United Church of Christ: A Guide to More Effective Church Membership. South Deerfield, Mass.: Channing L. Bete Company Inc., 1980.

A/G Facts, Current Information About the Assemblies of God. Springfield, Mo.: Gospel Publishing House, 1984.

Articles of Incorporation and Bylaws of the International Church of the Foursquare Gospel, (1986 edition). Los Angeles, 1986.

Bibliography

Assemblies of God, Who We Are and What We Believe. Springfield, Mo.: Gospel Publishing House, 1984.

Barrett, David, *The World Christian Encyclopedia*. New York: Oxford University Press, 1982.

Beacham, A.D. Sr. ed., *Minutes of the Twentieth General Conference of the Pentecostal Holiness Church Inc.* Franklin Springs, Ga.: Advocate Press, 1985.

Derstine, Gerald, *Champion of the Faith, Henry M. Brunk*. Bradenton, Fla.: Christian Retreat, 1985.

Facts You Should Know About the International Church of the Foursquare Gospel. Los Angeles: 1983.

Glick, Bishop Elam, "My Personal Pilgrimage" (Testimony, 1986).

Historical Data of the International Church of the Foursquare Gospel. April 1968.

Hollar, William, "The Charismatic Renewal in the Eastern Orthodox Church With Emphasis on the Logos Ministry for Orthodox Renewal" (M.A. thesis, Concordia Theological Seminary, Fort Wayne, Indiana).

Jacquet, Constance, *Yearbook of American and Canadian Churches*. Nashville: Abingdon Press, 1984.

Jones, Charles, *A Guide to the Study of the Holiness Movement*. Metuchen, N.J.: The Scarecrow Press, 1974.

————. *A Guide to the Study of the Pentecostal Movement*, 2 vols. Metuchen, N.J.: The Scarecrow Press, 1983.

Juillerat, L. Howard, *Book of Minutes, General Assemblies, Churches of God*. Cleveland, Tenn.: Church of God Publishing House, 1922.

Kenyon, Howard N., "Black Experience in the Assemblies of God" (Paper read at the Society for Pentecostal Studies, November 15, 1986, Costa Mesa, Calif.).

Koch, Roy, "The Hopewell Mennonite Church" (Manuscript).

Lee, Jae Bum, "Pentecostal Distinctives and Protestant Church Growth in Korea" (Ph.D. dissertation, Fuller Theological Seminary, 1986).

Lewis, Richard A., "E.N. Bell: An Early Pentecostal Spokesman" (Paper presented to the Society for Pentecostal Studies, November 4, 1986, Costa Mesa, Calif.).

Lewis, Warren, *Witnesses to the Holy Spirit*. Valley Forge, Pa.: Judson Press, 1978.

McDonnell, Kilian, *Presence, Power, Praise: Documents on the Charismatic Renewal*, 3 vols. Collegeville, Minn.: Liturgical Press, 1980.

Mansfield, Patti Gallagher, "Come, Holy Spirit" (Testimony read at the 1986 National Leaders' Conference, Steubenville, Ohio).

Manual/1985 Church of the Nazarene. Kansas City: Nazarene Publishing House, 1985.

Mennonite Renewal Services, Instrument for Renewal. Brochure, 1986. 3 p.

Melton, J. Gordon, *Biographical Dictionary of American Cult and Sect Leaders*. New York: Garland Publishing Company, 1986.

Mirly, Herbert, "Resurrection Lutheran Church, Charlotte, N.C." (Unpublished history, 1986).

Piepkorn, Arthur, *Profiles in Belief...Holiness and Pentecostal*, Vol. III. San

Francisco: Harper & Row Publishers, 1973.

Sawin, John S., "The Response and Attitude of Dr. A.B. Simpson and the Christian and Missionary Alliance to the Tongues Movement of 1906-1907" (Paper presented to the Society for Pentecostal Studies, November 4, 1986, Costa Mesa, Calif.).

Tanner, Paul, ed., "Report: Study Committee on Glossolalia" [Presented to the general assembly of the Church of God (Anderson, Indiana), June 18, 1986].

Wagner, C. Peter, "Survey of the Growth of the Charismatic Renewal" (Report, 1985).

Yawberg, Robert, *Diary*, April 24-26, 1978.

Yearbook, 1986, International Church of the Foursquare Gospel. Los Angeles: 1986.

Personal Interviews With the Author

Beatty, Bill
Bennett, Dennis
Bess, Ray and Marjorie
Bevis, Jim
Bartleman, Johnny
Black, Warren
Bonnke, Reinhard
Boone, Pat
Bradford, Brick
Brady, Dan
Brown, James H.
Buckingham, Jamie
Burns, Percy
Christenson, Larry
Cho, Paul Yonggi
Clark, Gary
Clemmons, Ithiel
Conn, Charles W.
Dayton, Donald
Derstine, Gerald
Dieter, Melvin
Dodge, Florence Adeline
Du Plessis, David
Durasoff, Steve
Emmert, Athanasios
Ervin, Howard

Flower, J. Roswell
Fullam, Everett L.
Gee, Donald
Ghezzi, Bert
Harper, Michael
Harrell, David
Helms, Harold
Hollenweger, Walter
Hoover, Mario
Hughes, Ray
Hunter, Harold
Jackson, Wilbur
Jones, Charles E.
Kendrick, Klaud
Koch, Roy
Lea, Larry
LeMaster, Don
Lovett, Leonard
Mansfield, Patti Gallagher
Martin, Leroy
Menzies, William
Moore, Charles
Mumford, Bob
Pethrus, Lewi
Ranaghan, Kevin
Martin, Ralph

Bibliography

McDonnell, Kilian
Menzies, William W.
Mirly, Herbert
Mjorud, Herbert
Montt, Efrain Rios
O'Connor, Edward
Osteen, John
Ostling, Richard
Parham, Pauline
Patterson, J.O.
Peters, John L.
Pfotenhauer, Donald
Ranaghan, Kevin
Roberts, Oral
Sandeen, Ernest
Shakarian, Demos
Simpson, Charles

Smith, Timothy
Stephanou, Eusebius
Stoop, Vernon
Suenens, Leon Joseph Cardinal
Synan, Joseph A.
Tomlinson, Milton
Urshan, Nathaniel
Vasquez, Javier
Wagner, C. Peter
Whetstone, Ross
Whitaker, Robert
Whitten, Clark
Wilkerson, David
Willis, Lewis J.
Winkler, Richard
Wogen, Norris
Voronov, Peter
Zimmerman, Thomas

227

Index

Index

231

Index

Index

Trinity Lutheran Church, 111, 118
Troccoli, Kathy, 61
Trogen, Larry, 171
Tyson, Tommy, 134, 135, 137

Unitarians, 174
United Church of Christ Renewal, 10, 173-179
United Holy Church, 7, 183
United Methodist Church, 135, 140
United Methodist Renewal Services Fellowship, 137, 141
United Pentecostal Church, 7

Vaagenes, Morris, 114, 117
Van Cleave, Nathaniel, 106
Vatican II, 45
"vision of the disinherited," 189
Voeks, George, 114

Wagner, C. Peter, 38
Walker, David, 141
Walker, Paul Lavern, 73
Walker, Robert, 32
Ward, C.M., 155
Warfield, B.B., 160
Watt, James, 23
Way of Faith, 150
Way of the Cross Lutheran Church, 114
Weiner, Bob, 8
Welch, John W., 21
Welcome, Holy Spirit, 115
Wesley, John, 131
Wesleyan Church, the, 138, 181
Wesleyan-Holiness Charismatic Fellowship, 187, 188
Wesleyan-Holiness Renewal, 10
Wesleyan Methodist Church, 182
Wesleyan Methodist Church of Brazil, 139, 157
Westburg, Wayne and Mary, 111
West Lauderdale Baptist Church, 35
Whetstone, Ross, 136, 141, 191, 192
Whitaker, Robert C., 166, 167, 171
White, Alma, 182
Whitten, Clark, 34, 35
Wilkerson, David, 40

Williams, J. Rodman, 169, 191
Williams, Roger, 27
Wimber, John, 34, 193, 194
Winkler, Richard, 6, 89, 92, 190
Wise, Robert, 171
Wogen, Norris, 115
Word and Witness, 18
"Word" churches, 8
Word of God community, The, 43, 46
World Christian Encyclopedia, 11, 51

Yawberg, Robert, 62, 63
Yoder, Allen, 125-126
Yoder, John Howard, 128
Yoido Full Gospel Church, 22
Young, D.J., 78
Youth With a Mission, 8
Yutzy, Dan, 126, 127

Zabrodsky, Boris, 146
Zimmerman, Thomas, 23